PEN

GENER.

D0720456

BAUDELAIRE IN ENGLISH

CHARLES-PIERRE BAUDELAIRE was born in Paris in 1821, the only son of an elderly father and young mother. His father died before he was six and his mother remarried a year later. Baudelaire was later to express violent hostility towards his stepfather, Colonel (subsequently General) Aupick. Wayward at school, he came second in the national Latin verse competition in 1837, but was still expelled from Lycée Louis-le-Grand in 1839. On his majority in 1842 he moved to a flat on the Ile St-Louis and indulged his artistic tastes so extravagantly that his parents, trying to safeguard what was left of his capital, transferred control of it to a lawyer, a well-meaning soul on whom Baudelaire would always vent his resentment at this humiliating situation.

Baudelaire was never again to be free from debt, or from schemes to restore his fortune by writing, publishing or lecturing. He suffered a stroke in Belgium in 1866, lingered on semi-paralysed and, latterly, mute and was brought back to Paris, where he died the following year. His collection of verse, *Les Fleurs du Mal* (1857), was the subject of a prosecution for indecency; six poems were removed from it and were not reinstated in France until 1949. Further editions, with more poems, appeared in 1861 and 1868. His prose poems and writings on art and literature were collected after his death; the literary criticism shows the influence of Edgar Allan Poe, whose short stories he also translated.

Baudelaire is known to have had attachments to three women, the longest-lasting to the creole Jeanne Duval. So far as we know he died childless.

CAROL CLARK is Fellow and Tutor in French at Balliol College, Oxford. She has also translated Baudelaire's *Selected Poems* for Penguin Classics.

ROBERT SYKES studied French and English Literature at Balliol College, and has taught French-English translation there. He is currently employed as a revising editor on the New Oxford English Dictionary project.

BAUDELAIRE IN ENGLISH

Edited by CAROL CLARK *and* ROBERT SYKES

PENGUIN BOOKS

PENGUIN BOOKS

Published by the Penguin Group
Penguin Books Ltd, 27 Wrights Lane, London w8 5tz, England
Penguin Books USA Inc., 375 Hudson Street, New York, New York 10014, USA
Penguin Books Australia Ltd, Ringwood, Victoria, Australia
Penguin Books Canada Ltd, 10 Alcorn Avenue, Toronto, Ontario, Canada m4v 3b2
Penguin Books (NZ) Ltd, 182–190 Wairau Road, Auckland 10, New Zealand

Penguin Books Ltd, Registered Offices: Harmondsworth, Middlesex, England

First published 1997
10 9 8 7 6 5 4 3 2 1

Copyright © Carol Clark and Robert Sykes, 1997
The acknowledgements on pages 259–62 constitute an extension of this copyright page
All rights reserved

The moral right of the editors has been asserted

Set in 10/12.5pt Monotype Bembo
Typeset by Rowland Phototypesetting Ltd, Bury St Edmunds, Suffolk
Printed in England by Clays Ltd, St Ives plc

CONTENTS

Harmonie du Soir 60

Bien loin d'ici   229

PETITS POÈMES EN PROSE

Epilogue   256

INTRODUCTION

Baudelaire is the first modern poet to figure in the 'Poets in Translation' series, and translating him, for the poets who attempted it, was a very different undertaking from measuring oneself against Horace, Virgil or the Psalms. To translate the Roman poets, to say nothing of the Psalmist, was to situate oneself within a tradition of authority. Horace, to quote Sir John Beaumont's verses prefixed to *Horace in English*, was 'this most usefull Poet'. 'The Latine writers' bred good in our minds by their labours: 'these strangers England with rich plentie feed'. For seventeenth-century and eighteenth-century Englishmen, Horace provided models of gentlemanliness. Baudelaire, on the other hand, has more typically provided models of alienation and transgression, first in his life and then in his writings. 'Horace' or 'Virgil' means to most readers chiefly a body of verse, handed down through time. 'Baudelaire' means first and foremost a person. Certainly we should have little interest in the person had he not left us his writings, but it is historically true that many of his readers, and many of those who went on to translate him, were first drawn to him by what they had learned of his life (often quite a garbled version of it). Almost every study of his poetry ever published begins with a biographical introduction, and we shall conform to this tradition.

Baudelaire was born in Paris in 1821 in the narrow, medieval rue Hautefeuille (the part of it now buried under the boulevard St-Germain) and baptized in the classical splendour of the church of St Sulpice. (He notes in his Journal how strong an impression was made on him as a child by the theatrical aspect of worship, and says that his ambition then was to be either the Pope or an actor.) His elderly father had trained for the priesthood but never practised, living instead as an artist and tutor to a noble family. In spite of this Baudelaire would boast, as a young man, of being under Heaven's curse as the son of a priest defrocked at the Revolution. His mother, born in London in 1793, the daughter of an *émigré* officer, had spent the first seven years of her life in England. No doubt it was from her that he first learnt English, which he knew unusually well for a Frenchman of his period (his translation of Poe's *Tales of Mystery and Imagination* is still the standard one). He appears, however, to have been more familiar with American poets (Longfellow, Poe) than with English ones.

Old M. Baudelaire died when Charles was nearly six; there followed a period of blissful intimacy with his mother which lasted hardly more than a year but coloured the rest of his emotional life. It was interrupted by his mother's remarriage to a man of her own age, a career army officer called Aupick. Commandant, later General, Aupick has been presented in English-language biographies of Baudelaire as a kind of Mr Murdstone, but this is unfair. He seems to have been a model officer, to have made his wife very happy and to have tried to understand his stepson and give him, by his lights, a good education. Baudelaire's letters suggest that, at least at first, he tried to please his stepfather, but without success. He was sent as a boarder first to the Collège Royal at Lyon, which he hated, and then to the Lycée Louis-le-Grand in Paris, where he was regarded as bright but wayward and eventually expelled. By the age of eighteen he was living in a boarding-house in the Latin Quarter supposedly studying law, but beginning to write and leading a mildly bohemian life. By this time he was expressing open hostility to his stepfather, and on one occasion picked a quarrel with him in Aupick's own house, before guests. To remove the boy from bad company, his parents decided to send him on a long sea voyage, but after five months he left the ship at Mauritius, and insisted on returning to France via La Réunion. He was not to leave Paris again for twenty-three years, apart from brief trips to visit his mother at Neuilly (then a village) and Honfleur.

At twenty-one he came into his inheritance from his father and moved to his own rooms on the Ile Saint-Louis, decorating them expensively and buying pictures and art objects. It was at this time that he began to move in artistic circles and became a friend of the older poet and critic Théophile Gautier, to whom *Les Fleurs du Mal* is dedicated. He was also, by this time, involved with Jeanne Duval, a woman of mixed race who had been a small-part actress but was soon to become wholly dependent on him and on other men. Within two years he had spent half of the capital which, wisely invested, would have given him a competence for the rest of his life. His desperate parents took the fateful step of giving him a *conseil judiciaire*: that is, of placing his remaining fortune under the control of a lawyer. This was to put Baudelaire in the legal position of a minor or a mental incompetent: he could no longer touch his capital except with the consent of M. Ancelle, who doled him out a (now much reduced) monthly allowance. This situation was to last for the rest of his life, with the result that the greater part of his correspondence is about money: begging letters to his mother, letters to possible publishers about money-making schemes that somehow never worked out, chilly missives to M. Ancelle written with an hauteur which fails to conceal his shaming position of dependence. Journalism brought in a few francs, but most of the time he dealt with debt simply by borrowing more money, at usurious rates.

By the time of the 1848 revolution, the twenty-seven-year-old Baudelaire's mode of life is settled. He has published his first poems and some art criticism, notably lengthy reviews of the Salons of 1845 and 1846; at this stage he often uses his mother's maiden name as well as his own to form the pen-name Baudelaire Dufaÿs. He lives at a bewildering succession of addresses, all in central Paris and all more or less sordid. He repeatedly breaks with Jeanne Duval, whom some of his friends facetiously refer to as *la Vénus noire*, only to take up with her again. In 1848 he is briefly caught up in left-wing politics, and it is said that during the June uprising he is seen rushing around in high excitement urging his hearers to come with him and kill General Aupick. But by October he is appointed editor of a conservative journal in the provinces. Taking the job would mean turning his back on Paris and after a few days he gives it up. After this his life changes little until 1864; we hear of the same seedy lodgings, from which he nevertheless emerges dressed with impeccable cleanliness; the same gentlemanly manners and quiet, hypnotic voice, even when he is recounting improbable and horrifying stories about himself; the eternal entanglement with the *Vénus noire*, whom he does not desert even when her looks are gone. There are other attachments to women: to Madame Sabatier, the beautiful, successful young *demi-mondaine* to whom he sends poems anonymously and with whom, after five years, he spends one night, followed by a letter of bitter regret; to Marie Daubrun, the green-eyed leading actress in whose life he probably played a very minor role. These attachments no doubt form the point of departure for the various 'cycles' of love poems in 'Spleen et Idéal' but these are surely based rather upon archetypes, on fantasies of womanhood, some of them characteristic of his period and others peculiar to the poet himself. The whole question of Baudelaire's sexuality is mysterious; at times he described himself in the hearing of strangers as a *pédéraste* (= homosexual, not paedophile) and some such suspicion seems to have hung over his expulsion from Louis-le-Grand. A close friend of his, Nadar the photographer, maintained that he never had complete sexual relations with any woman. An imaginative attempt at reconstructing his sexuality from his poems and journals underlies Angela Carter's short story, 'Black Venus'.

In 1855 Baudelaire's luck seemed to turn. Eighteen of his poems were published in the *Revue des deux mondes* and he began to discuss the publication of a single volume of all his poems written to that date. Undeterred by his mother's second bereavement in April 1857 he published *Les Fleurs du Mal* in June, opening it with the violently personal 'Bénédiction' in which he imagines the mother of the Poet looking in revulsion at her child, and saying that sooner than give birth to this '*monstre*', this '*dérision*', she would rather have dropped '*un nœud de vipères*' (a knot of vipers). (Mauriac took the title of his novel from this striking phrase.) His hopes that this volume would establish his literary reputation, and perhaps even make money, were immediately crushed. The whole edition was seized by the police, and Baudelaire and his publisher, Poulet-Malassis, put on trial for outraging public decency. They were convicted and fined in August and required to remove six poems from the book before distributing any more copies. The result was that very few copies were sold. By the 1860s Baudelaire is described as drinking to excess, though in an outwardly controlled fashion, and he himself refers in 'La chambre double' to his use of laudanum (opium prepared in drinkable form).

From 1859 to 1862 his artistic productivity increased, beginning with a series of working visits to his mother's house in Honfleur. As well as important critical articles, he wrote a whole new section, 'Tableaux parisiens', and other poems for a new edition of *Les Fleurs du Mal* which appeared in 1861, and began to work in a new genre, the prose poem. But artistic recognition and solvency seemed as far away as ever. His attempt to be elected to the Académie Française in 1861 was regarded with pained astonishment, and in 1864 he took the surprising decision to go to Belgium to give a series of lectures, which proved a disastrous failure. He hated Brussels (his last verses are satirical squibs against the dullness and personal dirtiness of its inhabitants), but he refused to return to Paris until he had found some way of clearing his debts. In March 1866 he collapsed in the church of Saint-Loup in Namur: partial paralysis was followed by further strokes which deprived him of the power of speech. (Later commentators have suspected the presence of tertiary syphilis.) He was brought back to Paris and lived on for a year in a nursing home, devotedly attended by his mother. Reconciled with the Church, so far as a mute man can be, he received the last rites and was buried with bourgeois decorum. He lies next to General Aupick.

It is clear that for readers in the puritanical societies of the Anglo-Saxon world before 1939 Baudelaire first represented the model of the intellectual bohemian: not one of the carefree characters of Murger or Du Maurier but a man sunk in dangerous dissipation and haunted by self-doubt and the fear of madness, what Verlaine was later to call a *poète maudit*. Laforgue, writing in 1885, could be offhand about Baudelaire's apparent excesses and speak of them as what Wilde would call a 'pose', adopted to keep the profane bourgeois at arm's length from his writing. He imagines Baudelaire saying

> Et d'abord pour éloigner le bourgeois, se cuirasser d'un peu de
>   fumisme extérieur . . .
> Aimer une Vénus noire, ou la Parisienne très-fardée.
> Abuser de parfums introuvables pour le lecteur.
> Parler de l'opium comme si on en faisait son ordinaire.
> Se décrire un intérieur peuplé de succubes.

Faire des poésies détachées, courtes, *sans sujet appréciable* . . . vagues et sans raison comme un battement d'éventail, éphémères et équivoques comme un maquillage, qui font dire au bourgeois que vient de lire 'Et après?'

[And first, so as to keep the bourgeois at a distance [I must] armour myself with a certain fake aura of mystery:

Love a black Venus, or the heavily-made-up Parisian woman.

Over-use perfumes the reader cannot get hold of.

Talk about opium as if it were my daily diet.

Describe a home life inhabited by succubae.

Write self-contained, short poems, with *no recognizable subject*, vague and unreasoning as the flutter of a fan, short-lived and equivocal as a stage make-up, which make the bourgeois say, when he gets to the end, 'Is that it?'][1]

However, for Swinburne, Symons or Crowley, Baudelaire's disregard of convention represents a real and heroic commitment. For such spirits, reading Baudelaire was a dangerous adventure, and to sympathize with him was to join an élite of the fearless. As Crowley writes in the preface to his translation of the *Petits Poèmes en prose*:

The thought of Baudelaire . . . has been universally recognized . . . as incompatible with any view of life which advocates spiritual complacency, mental and physical contentment. His writings are indeed the deadliest poison for the idle, the optimistic, the overfed. They must fill every really human spirit with that intense and insufferable yearning which drives it forth into the wilderness . . .[2]

But by the 1930s readers are more knowing, and Lewis Piaget Shanks can write in superior fashion that

American readers usually happen upon Baudelaire in college years, at some moment when boredom and penury send them to the library, to seek in books instead of life the Fruit of the Tree. Nibbled at surreptitiously without an adequate knowledge of French, *Les Fleurs du Mal* has for Anglo-Saxon boys a strange and sinister savour; they picture the poet as a romantic Ajax defying morals and convention . . .[3]

Under the influence of Freud, attention has now shifted to the dramas of Baudelaire's inner life. His contemporaries, and those elder writers like Sainte-Beuve who felt able to judge him, had all seen something faintly shameful in his inability, throughout forty years of life, to detach himself from the conflicts and habits of adolescence and even childhood. *Un pauvre garçon* is a phrase that recurs in their comments on him. His friends, like the poet himself, regarded his emotional life as something to be excused and, they hoped, transcended by the abiding achievement of his poetry. Not so some commentators of the 1930s, who regarded the drama of what would later be called 'the child within' as of continuing and consuming interest.

Readers of every period have read their own preoccupations into Baudelaire, as he saw men do into Nature:

> L'un t'éclaire avec son ardeur,
> L'autre en toi met son dueil, Nature!
> Ce qui dit à l'un: Sépulture!
> Dit à l'autre: Vie et Splendeur!

> [One man lights you up with his ardour
> The other puts all his mourning into you, o Nature!
> What says to the one, 'Burial!'
> Says to the other, 'Life and Splendour'!][4]

Poets born, like him, into the bourgeoisie (and nearly all of them were) have been fascinated by his attempts to break free from its values. His character as *poète maudit* has, since the Second World War, appealed chiefly to the young, while writers entering middle age, like Isherwood and Auden in 1947, when Isherwood's 1930 translation of the so-called *Intimate Journals* was reissued, have been moved by Baudelaire's attempts in his middle age to break with his self-destructive patterns of life and reassert the values of work and perseverance.

Isherwood's new preface to this translation is one of the most sympathetic pieces of biographical writing about Baudelaire ever done. It is followed by a new Introduction by Auden which is much more narrowly preoccupied with reclaiming Baudelaire for religion.[5]

Some of the late poems and personal writings do suggest that

Baudelaire in his forties returned to a form of highly idiosyncratic religious belief. One fragment, for example, under the heading 'Hygiène, Conduite, Méthode' expresses the resolve to pray every morning to God and to his own father, his old nurse and Edgar Allan Poe as intercessors with the deity. He prays for grace to achieve familiar objectives, solvency and reconciliation with his mother, but he seems now also to be aiming at a kind of personal redemption through poetic excellence.

Baudelaire may at one stage of his life have subscribed to the Romantic cliché that inspiration and glory were his birthright: now he sees salvation in temperate habits and unsparing work. There is certainly a poignant contrast between the serene Poet of 'Bénédiction', with his superior knowledge and insight ('*les vastes éclairs de son esprit lucide*') and his confidence that he will soon be seated among the choirs of angels wearing a crown of God's own fashioning, and the exhausted hack of 'A Une Heure du Matin' (*Petits Poèmes en prose* 10) who prays,

Seigneur mon Dieu! accordez-moi la grâce de produire quelques beaux vers qui me prouvent à moi-même que je ne suis pas le dernier des hommes, que je ne suis pas inferieur à ceux que je méprise!

[O Lord my God! give me the grace to produce a few good lines that will prove to myself that I am not the lowest of the low, that I am not inferior to those I despise.]

However, the accents of intellectual pride are still unmistakable. A confessor (and Baudelaire, so far as we know, never consulted one) would have said that the process of conversion still had a long way to go. In the event the promised life of sobriety and work proved as elusive as the 'lost jewels of ancient Palmyra'.

Les Fleurs du Mal and the *Petits Poèmes en prose* therefore stand as the testimony of Baudelaire's life, the useful harvest and beautiful flowers whose forms and colours will, perhaps, win the votes of the angels at the last day ('La Rançon', *Epaves* XIX). *Les Fleurs du Mal* is his only complete poetic work and it is as a complete work, a unity, that he wished it to be seen. On its first appearance the prose writer Barbey d'Aurévilly said in a review that

Les Fleurs du Mal do not simply follow one after another like so many lyric poems, produced by random inspiration and brought together for no other reason than to form a collection. They are not so much individual poems as a poetic work of the most powerful unity . . . They would therefore lose a great deal by not being read in the order in which the poet, who knows very well what he is doing, has placed them.[6]

Baudelaire strongly agreed; his first note to his defence counsel in his obscenity trial was, '*Le Livre doit être jugé* dans son ensemble' (The Book must be judged *as a whole*). The volume published in 1857 already has a strong structure, and in preparation for the 1861 edition Baudelaire reworked it, writing new material but also moving existing poems from one section to another to achieve a clearer artistic effect. It is for this reason that we have printed our selection of translations in the order in which the originals appear in the 1861 edition, and not chronologically.

The poems in the 1861 *Fleurs du Mal* are arranged in six sections, of greatly differing lengths. Following upon a deliberately insolent address 'Au Lecteur' (To the Reader), the longest section, 'Spleen et Idéal', opens with a score of poems which focus on the artist's life and calling; some of these made a strong appeal to his first translators, at a time when many were trying to define the role and personality of the artist and the relationship of poetry to the other arts.

There follows a long sequence of love poems which appear to fall into three cycles. French critics have baptized the first (XXIII–XXXIX), seemingly inspired by Baudelaire's long relationship with Jeanne Duval, the '*cycle de la Vénus noire*'. Then, apparently out of a desire for symmetry, they have distinguished a '*cycle de la Vénus blanche*' (XL–XLVIII) and even a '*cycle de la Vénus aux yeux verts*' (XLIX–LVIII). The 'white Venus' is identified with Mme Sabatier. This is reasonable in the sense that some of these poems were actually sent to her, in manuscript, as an anonymous gift. But the female figure celebrated in these poems – chaste, redemptive, angelic – has very little to do with the actual character of the beautiful, sociable, intelligent but far from chaste Mme Sabatier. (There survives a correspondence between her and Gautier, good-humoured but of the most breath-taking indecency.) It is doubtful whether even Baudelaire could have seriously believed in the Présidente as an angel and a madonna, and we may wonder whether 'A Celle qui est Trop Gaie' (*Épaves* v, but originally placed in this section) does not more accurately reflect his feelings for her.

In fact, in all the love poetry of 'Spleen et Idéal', but particularly in this section, the most striking characteristic is the intense lability of the feelings expressed. The female figure cursed and covered in vituperation in xxv or xxxi is the subject of nostalgic reflection in xxxviii and even undergoes a kind of apotheosis in xxxix. In xliv, the radiant health of the young woman addressed inspires only thoughts of redemption in the speaker, while in *Epaves* v the very same phenomenon sets off fantasies of sadistic revenge.

The third sequence of love poems (xlix onwards) is even harder than the others to assign to any particular relationship, though critics have tried. The characteristics of the female figure are muted, though the motif of green eyes does recur. She is addressed as mother, child and mistress and it is not clear whether she is present in reality or memory. She is associated with autumn, mists and uncertainty, world-weariness and approaching death. This sequence seems to end at poem lvi; numbers lvii to lxiii appear to be addressed to a variety of female figures, and reintroduce some of the sharp eroticism and sadistic themes of the first, '*Vénus noire*' group. A brief series of short poems on such disparate subjects as cats, owls or the poet's pipe separate the large body of love poems from the last and in many ways most interesting group of poems in 'Spleen et Idéal', that devoted to the Baudelairean leitmotif of *spleen*. This word, borrowed from English (see note, p. 84), is used to denote tedium, sloth, accidie, depression, but the feelings described can vary in intensity and emotional colouring from the quirkiness of 'Le Mort Joyeux' (The Happy Corpse, lxxii) or the first 'Spleen' (lxxvi) to the blackest gloom and the desire for personal annihilation (lxxvii, lxxix, lxxx, lxxxi). These poems with their psychological complexity, their modern, urban settings and strange, disparate imagery have exercised a particular fascination on translators from the 1950s onwards.

The following section, 'Tableaux parisiens', was added only in 1861. Its title recalls the *Scènes de la vie parisienne* of Balzac (whom Baudelaire greatly admired). But whereas Balzac's long novels are all solidly plotted, with the motivation of the characters established almost as carefully as their features and dress are described, the figures who flit through Baudelaire's urban landscapes are usually only touched in impression- istically. His relationship to them is that of the *flâneur*, of the man 'taking a bath in the multitude' as he would later say ('Les Foules', *Petits Poèmes en prose* 12). On this minimal, essentially safe level of engagement he can express, and perhaps feel, sympathy, though it is sympathy with joys and sorrows he has himself imagined ('Les Fenêtres', *PPP* 35). Several of his scenes are empty of other human beings (XCIX, CII); this is most notably true of LXXXVII, 'Le Soleil'. Under the beating sun, only the poet is out of doors; he seems to be weaving along like a drunkard (the real drunkard of CV, 'Le Vin des Chiffonniers' is described as staggering and bumping into walls 'like a poet'), but really he is working, practising ('m'exerçant'), sniffing out rhymes and tripping over words like uneven paving-stones, just once in a while stumbling upon the line he has been dreaming of. The identification of the poet with his distressed urban subjects is here complete, and this account of the poetic process is strikingly different both from the effortless sweep of the inspired poet of 'Bénédiction' and the purposeful, directed effort of 'L'Ennemi' (X) or 'La Rançon' (*Epaves* XIX).

The four short sections which conclude the *Fleurs du Mal* of 1861 are the same as in 1857: 'Le Vin', 'Fleurs du Mal', 'Révolte' and 'La Mort', but the long poem 'Le Voyage' which brings the volume to an end is again an addition of 1861. Curiously, given the reputation of poets, few of them have attempted translations of 'Le Vin' – perhaps because Baudelaire's attitude to wine is so characteristically French. For him wine is a positive force and intoxication with it usually healthy. It is associated with the sun, with hard, physical labour and an ordered, if brutish, life. The workman deserves his wine, whereas hashish, and still more opium, are bourgeois vices that demoralize the user and lead to artistic sterility. (These ideas are set out in his essays *Les Paradis artificiels*.) The anti-religious poems of 'Révolte' were written quite early and form a strong contrast with later ones like 'L'Imprévu' (*Epaves* XVIII) or 'La Rançon'. They have not often been translated, whereas those of 'La Mort' have inspired many versions.

The remainder of the collection lacks the clear structure of the 1861

Fleurs du Mal. As a result of the obscenity trial of 1857, six poems were excised from the collection; these were subsequently reprinted in 1866 in Belgium in an edition of 260 copies, together with seventeen other poems, some but not all newly composed. The title given to the whole was *Les Epaves* (*une épave* is a piece of flotsam or jetsam, an unclaimed object, a thing or person adrift), with subtitles 'Pièces Condamnées Tirées des Fleurs du Mal', 'Galanteries' (= poetic compliments), 'Pièces Diverses' and 'Bouffonneries' (= jokes). The whole series is numbered from I to XXIII and this edition has followed these numbers, but using small Roman type (i, ii, etc). Most of the *Epaves* were incorporated into the posthumous edition of *Les Fleurs du Mal* (1868), together with a handful of other pieces mostly written between 1861 and 1867. Baudelaire had not established any order for these, so we have followed that of the Pléiade edition (the standard modern edition), numbering them [I], [II], etc.

What judgement is a reader of the 1990s, or of the next century, likely to make of Baudelaire's poetic testament?

One must recognize that some of the subject-matter of the *Fleurs du Mal* has dated badly. It is not simply political correctness that makes modern readers, especially young women, turn in something like embarrassment from some of the love poetry. The extravagant power (so it seems to us) ascribed to women over their menfolk; the idea that by the mere fact of existing as a sexual and reproductive being a woman has a '*fangeuse grandeur! sublime ignominie!*' (XXV); the resolute coupling of sexuality and guilt (Baudelaire writes emphatically in *Fusées*, '*Moi, je dis: la volupté unique et suprême de l'amour gît dans la certitude de faire le mal*' – I say that the sole and supreme pleasure of sex lies in the certainty that we are doing *wrong*): all this is not so much shocking as almost incomprehensibly remote, a historical curiosity. Simone de Beauvoir prophesied in 1949, '*Peut-être le mythe de la femme s'éteindra-t-il un jour: plus les femmes s'affirment comme êtres humains, plus la merveilleuse qualité de l'Autre meurt en elles*' (Maybe the myth of woman will die out one day: the more women establish themselves as human beings, the more the magical quality of Otherness is dying in them), and it seems that half a century later her prediction has come nearer to being realized.

But when Baudelaire speaks of and for the isolated individual, the city-dweller, the old and poor and sad, many modern readers can more readily relate to him. Having been the poet of Art and Beauty and Sin for the decadents, of the psychologically troubled intellectual for the early moderns, he is perhaps particularly for us now the poet of the city.

Paris in his day was still the city of luxury trades, the earthly paradise (for the rich) that Voltaire had praised in 'Le Mondain'. It was not, and was never really to become, an industrial city – it consumed rather than produced. By the 1850s it was taking on its proverbial character as the international centre of pleasure and dissipation: 'gay Paris' in the old meaning of the word. But *gaîté parisienne* in Offenbach's sense is the last thing we find in Baudelaire's poems. Pleasure-seekers are excoriated with a preacher's old-fashioned eloquence:

> . . . si tu veux aujourd'hui
> Te pavaner aux lieux que la Folie encombre . . . (XXXVII)

> [if you wish, today,
> to parade in the places where Folly crowds . . .]

> le debris fumeux des stupides orgies (XLVI)
> [the smoky debris of crass orgies]

> Pendant que des mortels la multitude vile
> Sous le fouet du Plaisir, ce bourreau sans merci
> Va chercher des remords dans la fête servile ([VI])

> [While the vile throng of mortals, flying before the whip of Pleasure,
>   that merciless torturer, goes gathering remorse in the slavish
>   carnival]

Baudelaire's Paris is a city of memories, of dreams, of ghosts, '*où le spectre en plein jour accroche le passant*' (where ghosts in broad daylight catch the walker's sleeve, XC). To describe it, he develops a poetic language which mixes formal eloquence and irony, rapid shifts of register, even fleeting humour. Everywhere are strong and startling images, similes and metaphors which animate the city with human-like bodily fluids and what in his day would have been called 'electric' or 'magnetic' forces:

> Les mystères partout coulent commes des sèves
> Dans les canaux étroits du colosse puissant. (XC)

Four years after Baudelaire's death, Rimbaud decreed that the chief task of the poet was to *trouver une langue*, to find a new language able in some measure to transmit his privileged glimpses of the beyond. It was to Baudelaire that he turned as a model, crediting him with the power to '*inspecter l'invisible et entendre l'inouï* (inspect the invisible and hear the unheard-of) and calling him '*le premier voyant, roi des poètes*, un vrai Dieu' (the first seer, a king of poets, *a real God*). He added, however, that '*la forme si vantée en lui est mesquine*' (his much-praised form is petty-minded).

It is true that the patterns of argument, the unfolding of ideas in Baudelaire's poetry, his chosen vocabulary, similes and metaphors are ground-breakingly modern in a way his use of metre and rhyme are not. Yet he regarded mastery of these latter elements as crucial to his task of suggestion, and would certainly not have agreed to dispense with them and turn to something like free verse. (Nor did Rimbaud do so until the single late piece, 'Marine'.) What distinguishes Baudelaire as a writer of verse is the new fluidity and rhythmical subtlety he was able to give to the traditional metres, chiefly the alexandrine. This poses a particularly difficult task for the translator, who must choose between the iambic pentameter, which has the familiarity for English readers that the alexandrine has for the French but not its rigour, and the English alexandrine, an unwieldy affair that too often recalls Pope's 'wounded snake'. This problem is discussed below, pp. xl–xli.

Difficulties of translation on the level of vocabulary are touched on in the introduction to Baudelaire, *Selected Poems* (Penguin Classics, 1995). The only objective there was to produce an accurate prose version as an aid to reading the French text. Poetic translation is a different undertaking entirely, one which has room for daring cultural analogies: hence we find a used ashtray in Jeremy Reed's version of XXV, and young men in taxis in Laurence Lerner's of CIII. When Miss Havisham makes her appearance in Lerner's LXXVI, more doubts arise: such ready-made cultural references seem rather too easy, though when they are multiplied as in Nicholas Moore's many versions of LXXVII, one is dealing with a *tour de force* of a different kind. Some translators insist on making explicit the biographical references they think they see in veiled form in the original text. This trick of incorporating one's own footnotes is common and tiresome, as when translators cannot resist naming the '*négresse amaigrie et phthisique*' of LXXXIX as Jeanne Duval. For one thing, Jeanne, as we see in Manet's portrait of her, was not a negress but a pale mulatto – an important distinction in her native French West Indies. Another minor irritant regularly appearing even in good translations is what the French call 'false friends'. *Prairies* (IV) are not prairies but meadows, *baraques* (LXXXIX) not barracks but huts, and *enterrer* (CXII), *pace* Symons, certainly does not mean 'enter'! We have not commented on these inaccuracies except where they severely affect the sense of a translation.

The hardest thing for a translator to catch is the sheer simplicity of some of Baudelaire's lines. His favourite adjectives are the monosyllables *grand*, *doux*, *beau*, *bon*, and often whole phrases of a line or more have the rhythms and word order of everyday spech:

> Songe à la douceur
> D'aller là-bas vivre ensemble! (LIII)

> Andromaque, je pense à vous! (LXXXIX)

> Ma Douleur, donne-moi la main; viens par ici
> Loin d'eux ([vi])

Anything smacking of 'poetic diction' is death to lines like these. Baudelaire's *tu* is not the 'thou' of English verse aiming at loftiness, but the everyday *tu* used to a lover or a child. But flat, trivial, everyday English will not do either. It was of Racine that Sainte-Beuve said, '*Il rase la prose, mais avec des ailes*' (he skims the surface of prose, but upon wings); however, if we allow for a few more unexpected, more dangerous swoops, the observation could apply almost equally well to Baudelaire. This selection has shown a preference for poets who have captured this inspired plainness of Baudelaire's verse.

Baudelaire published poems in prose as well as verse, beginning in 1857 with six 'Poèmes Nocturnes'. They appeared in newspapers and literary magazines, and at the time of his first incapacitating stroke he was planning to publish a collection of them under the title *Le Spleen de Paris*. They were finally published together as volume IV of his complete works after his death, in 1869, under the title *Petits Poëmes en prose*. As they stand, they are a curiously disparate collection: some are scenes of Parisian life, some exchanges between a poet figure and a mistress (not always the same one), some lyrical and some satirically incisive in tone. A few are five or six pages long and could well be described as short stories, whether Wilde-like fables or revelations of human thoughtlessness, cruelty or perversity. They almost all include much more concrete, topical detail than the verse poems, but the style varies from one piece to another. In our selection we have concentrated on the shorter pieces in this collection, and on those which appear to offer parallel treatments of subjects also found in *Les Fleurs du Mal*. We have included, however, the notorious 'Assommons les Pauvres' (Smash the Poor), which gives us a glimpse of Baudelaire's politics towards the end of his life. The revolutionary of 1848 is now, if we can trust his personal notebooks, a reactionary, a disciple of de Maistre, contemptuous of all his century's promises of material and spiritual progress but yet not lacking in respect even for the most desperate of his co-dwellers in the great city.

*

The British public's awareness of contemporary French poetry was at nearly as low an ebb in the mid nineteenth century as at the end of the twentieth. The first publication of *Les Fleurs du Mal* appears to have passed without comment in the English press: it was not until the enlarged collection was reissued in 1861 that Algernon Charles Swinburne made its acquaintance and drew the attention of English readers to its author for the first time. His review, published in the *Spectator* in 1862, offered an enthusiastic welcome to an exponent of pure poetry willing to defy the middlebrow expectations of his native public. He commended Baudelaire's freedom from didacticism, and recognized with acuity the extent to which his poetry marked a movement beyond the bluster of the Romantic school to a more rhetorically controlled and probing pessimism: *Les Fleurs du Mal* 'has the languid, lurid beauty of close and threatening weather . . . It is quite clear of all whining and windy lamentation; there is nothing of the bubbling and shrieking style long since exploded. The writer delights in problems, and has a natural leaning to obscure and sorrowful things.'[7]

At the same time Swinburne was alert to defend Baudelaire against the charge of immorality still hanging over from the events of 1857, rejecting the view that the collection was riddled with paganism and primitivism with an assertion that 'there is not one of these poems that could have been written in a time when it was not the fashion to dig for moral motives and conscious reasons', and identifying a 'vivid background of morality' in the work as a whole. This seems like special pleading, especially since Swinburne goes on to single out 'Les Litanies de Satan' as 'in a way the keynote to this whole complicated tune of poems . . . one of the noblest lyrics ever written; the sound of it between wailing and triumph, as it were the blast blown by the trumpets of a brave army in irretrievable retreat' – an interpretation that would have done little to reassure the *bien-pensant* moralists who a decade later were to excoriate Baudelaire as a corrupting influence on English letters. Swinburne was clearly attracted by the revolutionary glamour of *Les Fleurs du Mal*, and the morality he detected in it was not the morality of Christian conformity, but rather a refusal of artistic compromise and an integrity of thought capable of withering the pretensions and hypocrisies of the bourgeois.

In the wake of such enthusiasm, it is disappointing that Swinburne did not produce any translations of Baudelaire. Even the French poet's influence on him is hard to track. There is a superficially Baudelairean tone in his *Poems and Ballads* (1866), but many of the pieces predate his reading of *Les Fleurs du Mal*; his admiration for de Sade seems to have been at least as important to his exploration of the imagery of submissive sexuality. Thereafter his work becomes more political in tone and any obvious influence fades away; although his elegy 'Ave atque Vale' (1867), written on the (premature) news of Baudelaire's death, makes clear the strength of his continuing admiration.

As more and more British writers and critics felt impelled to take

sides over the question of 'Art for Art's sake', so Baudelaire's name
began to appear more frequently in the literary reviews, either cited as
an aesthetic exemplar or demonized as a dangerous immoralist – at first
more frequently the latter, as Swinburne's advocacy had unwittingly
alerted the thought police of the time to the existence of a useful
scapegoat. The critic and poetaster Robert Buchanan made a virulent
if laboured attempt to blame the prurience of modern literature ('Leg-
literature') for the moral degeneracy of society as a whole in his diatribe
The Fleshly School of Poetry (1872), in which Baudelaire and D. G.
Rossetti are accorded a chapter each as chief villains. Having prepared
the ground by dismissing love poetry in general as 'the Italian disease',
lately replenished by 'a fresh importation of the obnoxious matter from
France', Buchanan launches into a spitefully jingoistic and largely fanciful
attack upon Baudelaire's personal qualities. Baudelaire was a 'poor,
attenuated, miserable scarecrow of humanity' whose 'reading, which
seems to have been of a very limited nature, developed his already
singular disposition into true literary monstrosity'; into his mouth are
put the words of some parodic Hellfire Club freethinker: ' " What
poetry is to life, the drug hasheesh is to me personally, enabling me to
extract supreme enjoyment out of the sheerly diabolical ideas of my
own mind. I despise humanity, and I approve the devil." ' Buchanan
then proceeds to call for what amounts to an import ban on diseased
poetry, before the native stock succumb to wholesale infection: 'All
that is worst in Mr Swinburne belongs to Baudelaire. The offensive
choice of subject, the obtrusion of unnatural passion, the blasphemy,
the wretched animalism, all are taken intact out of the "Fleurs de
Mal"[*sic*]. Pitiful! that any sane man, least of all an English poet, should
think this dunghill worthy of importation!' Invoking a favourite penny-
shocker image of Parisian decadence, 'This poetry,' concludes Buch-
anan, 'is like absinthe, comparatively harmless perhaps if sipped in small
quantities well diluted, but fatal if taken (as by Mr Swinburne) in all its
native strength and abomination.' Swinburne, now on his way back to
poetic health, is clearly lucky to have been able to shake off the addiction,
and is to be held up as an awful example to any young English poet
contemplating a visit to the fleshpots of Paris.

Buchanan's analyses of actual poems make it clear that his French was poor and his knowledge of the work cursory, but these details hardly mattered, such was the general unfamiliarity with French poetry. Despite the occasional ripostes of more liberal critics (most notably an acute and sympathetic assessment by George Saintsbury in the *Fortnightly Review*, XXIV, 1875, deploring the philistines' appropriation of Baudelaire as 'a sort of spiritual Aunt Sally' and insisting upon the vital importance of *Les Fleurs du Mal* as an 'anatomy' of the 'modern cultivated mind' and its fatal propensity to ennui), still the cumulative effect of the lurid attacks was to ensure that for many years, when Baudelaire was translated at all, it was usually a matter of including versions of one or two of the less challenging pieces amid a collection of original verse, as if to add a little whiff of absinthe. Such was the case with the translations by R. H. Shepherd (1869), Arthur Reed Ropes (1882), Eugene Mason (1890) and Margaret Jourdain (1911). Others such as Henry Curwen (1870), W. J. Robertson (1895) and John Payne (1906) included versions of Baudelaire in anthologies of French poetry in translation, showing at least that English writers who took a professional interest in French literature were willing to accord him a place alongside other established figures.

   The first sizeable selection of Baudelaire in English, marketed as such and not interpolated into a collection of original poetry, did not appear until 1894. This was *Some Translations from Charles Baudelaire, Poet and Symbolist* by one 'H. C.', generally identified as the Henry Curwen who had included two Baudelaire pieces in his *Echoes from French Poets*, 1870 (although these later pieces are stylistically so different that one can only wonder about the likelihood of the attribution). H. C., whoever he or she might be, presents an extensive selection from *Les Fleurs du Mal*, fifty-three poems in all, although weighted somewhat in favour of the more straightforward and easily translated sonnets and shorter lyrics and away from the darker and more philosophical pieces. Many of these versions, it must be admitted, give a fairly superficial impression of their originals: on a literal level they are generally quite accurate, but suffer in common with most of the translations of this period from an over-reliance on conventional poetic language – inversions, archaisms of vocabulary and so on – which seems, at least to modern eyes, to transmit the poise and precision of Baudelaire's diction through a soft-focus filter.

Over the next fifteen years this modest advance was consolidated with the publication of three further noteworthy selections and a handful of individual translations. One might have expected that Baudelaire's growing posthumous notoriety as dandy, debauchee and narcomane, not to say, on a more serious level, his reputation as a paragon of dedicated and uncompromising artistry, would have constituted an instant recommendation to the Decadent writers of the last years of the century, but this kinship gave rise to little in the way of translations. Poets such as Ernest Dowson and John Gray (who included three rather unsatisfactory Baudelaire versions in *Silverpoints*, 1893) displayed more interest in relatively recent French writers closer to Symbolism, in particular Verlaine and Rimbaud. The importance of Baudelaire to the birth of the Symbolist movement was a disputed point, and the Symbolist approach was increasingly seen as the valid one for contemporary writing. Arthur Symons in his *The Symbolist Movement in Literature* (1899) considers Gérard de Nerval in depth as the godfather of the movement, while dismissing Baudelaire in a sentence as part of the Realist tendency against which the later movement was a reaction: 'Baudelaire, in whom the spirit is always an uneasy guest at the orgy of life, had a certain theory of Realism which tortures many of his poems into strange, metallic shapes, and fills them with imitative odours, and disturbs them with a too deliberate rhetoric of the flesh' – an oddly superficial judgement that he had certainly revised by 1918, when he produced two enthusiastic articles about Baudelaire (incorporated in a book-length study two years later)[8] and perhaps even by 1905, when he published a small but intriguing selection of translations from the *Petits Poèmes en prose*, the first to appear in English. Much later, Baudelaire's 'rhetoric of the flesh' was to become the keynote of Symons's extraordinary 1925 translation of *Les Fleurs du Mal* (see below), a belated and stillborn offspring of the relationship between the former's complex pessimism and the satanic posturings of the English *fin de siècle*.

Among the few other translations to arise directly from the Decadent milieu were a single version (of 'La Destruction') by Vincent O'Sullivan, a Francophile American friend of Oscar Wilde, and four by Lord Alfred

Douglas. Douglas chose as subjects for his first two translations (printed in his collection *The City of the Soul*, 1899) the patterned, repetitive ecstasies of two of Baudelaire's lushest evocations of swooning love nostalgia, 'Harmonie du Soir' and 'Le Balcon'. Douglas's two later translations of sonnets (1909) show a much more developed understanding; but by this time two selected translations of considerable merit had appeared from very different poets. The first, Frank Pearce Sturm's *The Poems of Charles Baudelaire*, 1906, still deserves to be considered among the most successful attempts to render a sizeable selection of the oeuvre, and moreover marks the birth of an interest in Baudelaire among the proponents of that esoteric movement which was reaching beyond the rather superficial occult explorations of the Decadent circle (see p. 27 for a note on Sturm's involvement with esotericism and his friendship with Yeats) – a sympathy which would bear further fruit in translations by Aleister Crowley, Cyril Scott (not represented here) and Yeats's friend Thomas Sturge Moore. Sturm's translation (although produced to a commission) shows a deep engagement with his subject, evidenced not only in the poems themselves but also in his perceptive and thought-provoking introduction, which suggests a long familiarity with Baudelaire on his part. His selection of poems, while still avoiding the potentially scandalous material, is more rounded than H. C.'s, including cogent versions of some of the longest and most taxing pieces, such as 'Le Cygne' and 'Le Voyage' – his translation of the latter remains the most convincing that has been done.

The analysis of Baudelaire ('Charles Baudelaire: a Study') which forms the introduction to Sturm's selection deserves close attention. Sturm's conception of the transcendental nature of Baudelaire's sensuality and the transfiguring capacity of genuine decadence is so convincing as to be worth quoting at length:

Charles Baudelaire was one of those who take the downward path which leads to salvation. There are men born to be the martyrs of the world and of their own time; men . . . who are so intoxicated with a vision of a beauty beyond the world that the world's beauty seems to them but a little paint above the faces of the dead; who love God with a so consuming fire that they must praise evil for God's glory. . .; and because the good and evil in their souls finds a so perfect instrument in the refined and tortured body of modern times, desire keener pleasure and more intolerable anguish than the world contains . . . Baudelaire *is* decadence; his art is not a mere literary affectation, a mask of sorrow to be thrown aside when the curtain falls, but the voice of an imagination plunged into the contemplation of all the perverse and fallen loveliness of the world . . . All his life Baudelaire was a victim of an unutterable weariness, that terrible malady of the soul born out of old times to prey upon civilizations that have reached their zenith . . . he took his revenge upon life by a glorification of all the sorrowful things that it is life's continual desire to forget.

Sturm's analysis prophetically suggests to a present-day reader the extent to which Baudelaire's descent into an urban hell is a crucial precursor of Modernism, and the Decadent movement a mere preliminary sketch for the Modernist programme – indeed Sturm's own language is suggestive of that nascent movement's concern with the phenomenon of over-civilization and the need for a purgatorial renewal of the social body. He appears to have been the first writer in English to notice just how central to Baudelaire and to his importance for future generations are the sense of the simultaneous beauty and unnaturalness of modern urban life, and the notion of the possibility of individual redemption through and only through an engagement with the compromises of the flesh, a baptism in sin. In Sturm's view, it was impossible to overestimate the influence that *Les Fleurs du Mal* had had on Western society in the half-century since its first publication: 'The change wrought, directly or indirectly, by *The Flowers of Evil* . . . is almost too great to be properly understood. There is perhaps not a man in Europe today whose outlook on life would not have been different had *The Flowers of Evil* never been written' – although he harbours no illusions about the debased form in which the work's ideas had been transmitted 'by the lesser writers who labour for the multitude', pooh-poohing the English Aesthetes with their mission 'to preach the gospel of imagination to the unimaginative', and dismissing Swinburne's Baudelaireanisms as 'wan derivatives . . . where Baudelaire compresses some perverse and morbid image into a single unforgettable line, Mr Swinburne beats it into a froth of many musical lovely words'.

It is in Symbolism that Sturm considers the revolution begun by

Baudelaire has finally borne fruit: but Sturm's Symbolism is a subtler creature than Symons's, and his analysis of Baudelaire's relation to it altogether more intricate. Symbolism as Sturm presents it is a faith – somewhat akin to Neoplatonism in its insistence on the flimsy and deceptive nature of the material order and the importance of the imagination as the means to spiritual revelation. He is aware that this faith does not correspond exactly to Baudelaire's beliefs, but presents Baudelaire's materialism as a telescoped proto-Symbolism: 'Sound, colour, odour, form: to him these are not the symbols that lead the soul towards the infinite: they are the soul; they are the infinite' – a profound understanding, even if Sturm's pro-Symbolist viewpoint kept him from recognizing Baudelaire's position as yet more radical than that of the movement that succeeded him.

The sympathy evident in this essay is by and large well reflected in Sturm's translations, which (except for those poems, such as 'Le Balcon', where a hypnotic musicality is required) have a firmness and simplicity of language far removed from the poeticisms of most of the earlier versions. Only his renderings of the prose poems (of which he prints a fair selection) disappoint – here his clear prose becomes awkward and vaguely archaic, perhaps reflecting an overzealous attempt to square up to his estimation that 'Some of them . . . are as classical and as universally true as the myths and symbolisms of the Old Testament.'

Three years after Sturm's ground-breaking edition, another selection from *Les Fleurs du Mal* appeared in the shape of *Poems and Baudelaire Flowers*, the first collection of original poetry by the young J. C. Squire, about two thirds of which is devoted to translations from Baudelaire. Squire, who never declared an allegiance to Decadent or Symbolist circles, and who is remembered nowadays as a clubbable all-round man of letters, influential reactionary critic and writer of pleasant, undemanding verse, may seem a surprising figure to be nailing his youthful colours to Baudelaire's mast: that he should do so indicates perhaps that the publications of the preceding years were at last beginning to roll back the tide of opprobrium and make Baudelaire an almost respectable interest. None the less Squire's selection does not shun the dark and difficult side of *Les Fleurs de Mal* quite as much as H.C.'s or Sturm's: he squares up to the squalid scenario of 'Une nuit que j'étais . . .', and offers a largely successful rendering of 'Un Voyage à Cythère'. His manner is a little more ornate and 'poetic' than Sturm's, but the stylistic sensitivity that would later make him a renowned parodist is already in evidence, as he responds to the swooning ecstasies of 'La Chevelure' with a rich, sonorous vocabulary, to the gentle murmur of 'L'Invitation au Voyage' with language of a calm simplicity and exquisite rhythmical poise, or with harsh, blunt words to the horror of 'L'Aube Spirituelle' or 'Quand le ciel bas et lourd . . .' Here, as frequently in Sturm's translations, and also in Douglas's two 1909 sonnets and James Elroy Flecker's 'Litany to Satan' of a few years later, we sense real poetic sensibilities at last coming to grips with Baudelaire.

The Great War inevitably led to a hiatus in literary translation as writers turned to more pressing concerns; but in the ensuing poetic landscape of directness and growing linguistic experimentalism, we might expect to see Baudelaire vindicated as a prophet of the modern sensibility – an expectation not to be fulfilled immediately, however. The first new translation by a poet of any importance to appear after the war, apart from Allen Tate's 1924 version of 'Correspondances', was Arthur Symons's 1925 edition of the verse and prose poems together with part of *Les Paradis artificiels*. Presented as the first complete translation of the poet's work (in fact Symons translated the first, 1857, edition of *Les Fleurs du Mal*, thus omitting a number of the best-known pieces), this should have been a landmark, and Symons's spirited earlier selection from the prose poems would have given anyone who recalled it grounds for considerable expectation; but a reader who had studied his two more recent articles or his short book of 1920 might have come armed with misgivings. It seems that Symons had begun to revisit with an immoderate enthusiasm the Decadent habits of his youth. In the *English Review* of January 1918 he wrote:

Baudelaire's genius is satanical; he has in a sense the vision of Satan . . . He sees the vanity of the world with finer modern tastes than Solomon; for his imagination is abnormal, and divinely normal . . . His soul swims on music played on no human instrument, but on strings that the Devil pulls, to which certain living puppets dance in grotesque fashion . . . to the sound of violins strummed on by evil spirits in Witches' Sabbatts [*sic*].

Symons's characterization of Baudelaire as 'material by passion, Christian by perversity' has some truth in it, and he makes some intelligent observations upon the abstract nature of Baudelaire's language ('there is no intrusion of words used for the irrelevant purpose of describing') and the particular modernity of this characteristic; but despite his perspicacious awareness (in the 1920 study) of the *precision* of Baudelaire's phantasmagoria ('the almost medical curiosity of certain researches into the stuff of dreams, the very fibre of life itself'), it is his own wild and nostalgic flights of satanic fancy which unfortunately set the tone of his subsequent translations. As T. S. Eliot remarked in a review of the collection, 'Baudelaire becomes a poet of the nineties – and not a good one at that.'[9]

In 1908 Symons had suffered a mental breakdown followed by near-death from pneumonia, and the critical consensus that he never thereafter regained his earlier abilities is sadly and amply borne out by this collection: with the honourable exception of most of the prose poems (which may perhaps date from the period of his original selection, although not then published) they are quite simply among the worst translations of any original ever produced in English by a reputable poet. Symons's method is to bolster up the existing sense with whatever additional imagery – metaphors or epithets plucked from elsewhere in Baudelaire, gratuitous references to Satan – he feels will add an air of authenticity. Often this improvisation is inspired by the necessity of supplying a rhyme; just as often it appears to be caprice – in too many cases rhyme and metre go rattling on in a way that calls to mind the works of William McGonagall.

All of this would be scarcely worth remarking upon were it not for the fact that Symons's translation was widely accepted as 'the official representative of Baudelaire in English', in the words of Jackson Mathews, who goes on to describe it as 'the book that has put Baudelaire among those lurid authors whose works are most often "missing" from the public libraries'.[10] It is hard to know how this came to be so: certainly Symons was a poet of reputation, but by 1925 few would have considered him at the forefront of his art. If, as Mathews suggests, Symons's version merely chimed in with the racy spirit of the times, one might have expected it to inspire a flurry of new versions; in fact the only further inter-war collections were produced in the United States, where Symons's baleful influence may have been moderated by the continued availability of a pirated, uncredited 1919 edition of Sturm's translations. It seems more likely that Symons's version, as far as it had any influence in Britain, helped to revive the misconception of Baudelaire as a posturing diabolist and to persuade serious readers that he must really be unworthy of attention. At any rate, he was not as strong a presence in British letters between the wars as he had been two and three decades previously: a number of critical and biographical studies appeared (most notably Enid Starkie's celebrated biography of 1933), but his literary influence was largely confined to francophone cognoscenti such as T. S. Eliot and Aldous Huxley, who chose to use him as a reference point in their definitions of the modern experience. Huxley in his early fiction deploys a negative image of Baudelaire as the type of the splenetic, life-denying cynic – see in particular *Point Counter Point*, where Baudelairean imagery of the damned poet and nihilist is extensively invoked in the character of the misanthrope Spandrell. Yet he also produced a masterly translation of one of Baudelaire's superficially most decadent (yet also most aggressively moral) poems, a poem exhibiting precisely that morbid pessimism, that fascinated exploration of extreme experience followed by a turning away in spiritual disgust or moral defeat, which he satirizes in his fiction but which gives the keynote, at differing levels of seriousness, to a number of his most telling characters. Eliot on the other hand drew heavily on Baudelaire's Parisian imagery, in *The Waste Land* and elsewhere – and affirmed Baudelaire's influence, both upon himself and upon the whole urban programme of modern writing, in his essay 'Baudelaire' of 1930: 'It is . . . not merely in the use of imagery of the sordid life of a great metropolis, but in the elevation of such imagery to the *first intensity* – presenting it as it is, and yet making it represent something much more than itself – that Baudelaire has created a mode of release and expression for other men.'[11] This specifically Baudelairean 'mode' he defined elsewhere as 'the possibility of fusion between the sordidly realistic and phantasmagoric'[12] – the sort of fusion undertaken, in a similarly urban context and with an awareness of Eliot's decisive example, by writers as diverse as Virginia Woolf and Charles Williams. We may, then, consider Eliot as the channel through which Baudelaire's poetry of the city helped to fecundate the important urban-metaphysical strain in British writing between the wars.

By contrast with this period of relative neglect by British poets, the interest of their American colleagues in Baudelaire appears to have grown between the wars: a number of young writers such as Allen Tate and Hart Crane tracked back through the Symbolists and came upon Baudelaire, who became a potent figurehead for their own aesthetic or spiritual emancipations. In general, though, this was a youthful enthusiasm which bore a limited relation to the mature direction of their poetry – and produced little in the way of translations compared to the abundance that was to follow after the Second World War. The first substantial American collection (1926) came not from a poet but from a Professor of French Literature, Lewis Piaget Shanks. Shanks, fortunately, was a far-from-dry academic: his translations, though sometimes marred by old-fashioned language, just as frequently impress with intense, compressed syntax and modern-sounding enjambements and rhymes on function-words, often producing a poetry more urgent and less poised than the original, but one which gives the impression of actually having been experienced and conceived afresh, and allows us to forget that we are reading a translation (his splendid version of 'Le Flacon', p. 64, exemplifies this curious old-new fluency). Jackson Mathews describes Shanks as 'the first translator who tried, by bold and honest reading, to bring into English the whole lower register of Baudelaire's tone' – that register which Huxley was invoking in his anatomies of present-day nihilism, which Sturm had recognized but had transmitted to only a limited extent, and which Symons had garbled only the previous year into a farrago of melodramatic naughtiness. For this frank and unsensationalistic approach and for the immediacy of his language at its best, Shanks deserves to be called the first modern translator of Baudelaire.

A similar directness and a receptiveness to the full range of Baudelaire's vision mark the selection translated jointly by George Dillon and Edna St Vincent Millay and published in 1936. In her preface Millay presents Baudelaire not merely as an abstract icon of modernity but as a typical city-dweller whose experiences are immediately referable to those of present-day urbanites: 'His pleasures were found in those amenities which the city affords . . .: handsome architecture; exhibitions of paintings and etchings . . .; elegant ladies wearing furs and jewels and smelling of synthetic perfumes . . . New York as a spectacle would have delighted him.' She was the first translator to latch on to this celebratory and lyrical aspect of Baudelaire's relationship with the city, and her translations from the *Tableaux Parisiens* are notably successful. She ranges Baudelaire's perfectionism and intellectual precision alongside his awareness of universal stupidity and his moods of impotent despair ('his mind that could not go mad, although, as he says, equipped with all the machinery for going mad'), and insists on an image of him very far removed from that of the Decadents: not an intellectual flagellant, of himself or of humanity as a whole, but a humanist, a 'subtle and balanced mind' who 'hated all that *de*bilitated, *de*feated, *de*stroyed the majesty of the human mind' and who 'proposed to conquer ugliness by making beauty of it'. Her scorn for those translators who, misunderstanding this process and shying away from Baudelaire's more demanding confrontations with ugliness and sin, 'translate him with the lights out', is reinforced with versions of some of his most shocking poems, such as her rendering of 'Une Martyre' and Dillon's of 'Le Vin de l'Assassin'.

Elsewhere in her preface Millay expresses a strong interest in formal aspects of translation, and in particular in the choice of metre to render Baudelaire's alexandrines: she confesses that she was drawn to the project in part because of Dillon's insistence that an alexandrine should be rendered by an alexandrine – whereas the majority of previous translators had adopted as a matter of course the five-stressed, more-or-less iambic, more-or-less decasyllabic line which has been the workhorse of English poetry from the sixteenth century onward. It does not take a prosodist to realize the naïvety of this literal-minded attempt at absolute mimesis, for all Millay's impassioned exposition of it as the only way to produce a translation which is 'still, in some miraculous way, the same poem'. In the first place, as she seems to have half-realized, English prosody works as much by stress as by syllable count: there is arguably no such thing as an English alexandrine. She does admit that they are actually working with iambic hexameters, but goes on to explain how they have striven to rein in the strong accents of English words in pursuit of the sound of French verse, apparently unaware of the incompatibility of this aim with her laudable wish that the translator 'must feel, at least during the period at which he is at work upon [the poem], that he might have written it himself . . . must . . . fill the veins of the poem . . . with his own blood, and make the poem breathe again'. Furthermore, as Jackson Mathews trenchantly observes, 'In the history of English poetry the hexameter has been an eccentric line, whereas the alexandrine is the central "heroic" line of French poetry', so that any translation into hexameter misses the traditionalist formal impulse that runs in counterpoint to Baudelaire's radical subject–matter. The length of the line militates, too, in favour of a certain prolixity, which at times assists Millay's wry conversational tone but also weakens the imagery of the originals by the importation of redundant epithets and locutions. Dillon meanwhile attempts to vitalize the longer lines by varying stress and number of syllables but, lacking Millay's metrical control, sometimes produces clumsy renderings.

Millay's prolixity is much less apparent in her translations of originals with shorter or irregular lines, which in any case are often those where her quixotic voice seems most at home (for example 'Ever So Far from Here' (p. 231), with its overtones of Dorothy Parker). Indeed, one of the most satisfying aspects of this collection is the way in which Millay's detached, ironic persona succeeds in inhabiting some of Baudelaire's more reflective and nostalgic poems and, without traducing his meaning, imbues them with a distinctly female and very American character. Another example is 'The Sphinx' ('J'ai plus de souvenirs . . .') where she expands Baudelaire's opening line into a splendidly laconic couplet, maintains this tone of wry self-deprecation through the following section, but then gradually tightens up her rhetoric (for all that she introduces a few extra images) to an appropriately grand and desolate peroration. With such a gift for combining a translator's fidelity of spirit with that essential transfusion of poetic lifeblood, one can only wonder at her enthusiasm for Dillon's dogmatic metrical purism, which bespeaks an altogether less evolved conception of translation than that suggested by her own practice. We must regret, too, that her example has not inspired many more women to translate Baudelaire: the ambiguous presentation of woman in his poetry must act as a disincentive, but surely also offers possibilities for all manner of ironic and deconstructive approaches.

These questions of the translator's responsibility to the work translated, of the degree of freedom permissible or desirable, of the whole purpose and scope of the act of translation, become increasingly relevant to the versions of Baudelaire produced since the Second World War. In part, this is a reflection of growing debate about the nature of poetic translation as a whole, and the assimilation of the idea of free imitation as a basis for original expression put forward by Ezra Pound and others. But it also implies that Baudelaire's poetry was now becoming a recognized enough feature of the anglophone literary scene for such liberty to be practicable. After all, the pedigree of free translation and adaptation in English can be traced back through Dryden and Shakespeare to the Middle Ages; but when it becomes a matter not merely of mining source material but, as increasingly conceived by modern translators, of exploiting an ironic relationship between original and translation, then it is essential that the translator's readership have at the very least a clear received idea of the original author's concerns, and preferably some first-hand familiarity with his work.

The two collections last discussed had played their part in this process of familiarization, as had the publication in 1940 by the Limited Editions Club of an edition of *Les Fleurs du Mal* which rounded up work by the majority of Baudelaire's translators to date, including a quantity of unpublished versions, notably those by Sir Eric Maclagan, and a number specially written by the editor, James Laver. Notwithstanding Laver's perspicacious editing, it is probably fair to say that the American public of this time was more at home with Baudelaire than the British; at any event the majority of the translations that were to appear until the late 1960s were American. In 1950, Arthur Kraetzer even offered an edition of *Les Fleurs du Mal* 'translated literally into verse . . . with psychoanalytic notes'. Alongside such earnest dissections of the poet's subconscious impulses, Alan Conder's version, one of two complete translations published in England in 1952, reads a little quaintly, with a mellifluousness reminiscent of Squire. Conder (a noted violinist) was sixty-eight when his volume appeared, and it is not surprising that he should fall back on the poetic mode of a more settled age.

Roy Campbell's edition of the same year offers an altogether more forceful and energetic interpretation: though working, like F. P. Sturm, to a commission, he had (as presumably had Sturm) a long-standing attachment to Baudelaire's work, and – much more than Sturm or even Symons – identified himself with his subject's emotions and experiences. In the words of his prefatory note: 'I have been reading Baudelaire since I was fifteen, carried him in my haversack through two wars, and loved him longer and more deeply than any other poet. I translated St John of the Cross because he miraculously saved my life in Toledo in 1936. I am translating Baudelaire because he lived my life up to the same age, with similar sins, remorses, ostracisms, and poverty, and the same desperate hope of reconciliation and pardon.'

Much of Campbell's earlier verse, particularly pieces in his first collection of short poems *Adamastor* (1930) and its successor *Flowering Reeds* (1933), contains strong echoes of Baudelaire. In *Adamastor*, for example, 'The Making of a Poet' takes up the image of poet as outcast presented in 'Bénédiction' and 'L'Albatros'; 'The Serf', like 'Le Squelette Laboureur' and 'Le Crépuscule du Matin', considers the ancient, inexorable burden of the poor's labour; and in 'The Zulu Girl' a young Zulu mother 'looms above' her suckling infant 'as a hill/Within whose shade a village lies at rest' and nourishes him with 'An old unquenched unsmotherable heat –/The curbed ferocity of beaten tribes,/The sullen dignity of their defeat' – a rich convergence of Baudelairean imagery, most obviously suggestive of 'La Géante' and 'Bohémiens en Voyage' but more generally drawing on the favourite topos of the pride and resilience of the exiled and vanquished ('Don Juan aux Enfers', 'Les Litanies de Satan', etc.). *Flowering Reeds* contains a translation of 'L'Albatros' and further reworkings of Baudelairean material: two poems, 'The Flame' and 'Wings', take the ecstatic imagery of 'La Chevelure' as a point of departure, while 'Overtime' ingeniously reworks 'Le Squelette Laboureur' with echoes of 'Une Gravure Fantastique' and 'Danse Macabre'.

Campbell's personal engagement lends considerable power especially to his versions of the harsher, more pessimistic poems. Himself an extrovert, a lover of extremes, a Catholic convert of decidedly pagan bent, he was drawn, in George Steiner's words, 'to Baudelaire's *morbidezza*, to the nervous strength and dandyism of his manner'[13] as much as to those themes of heroic struggle and exile that chimed with his own experience (some would say his assiduously cultivated persona) as a maverick South African outsider in the haughty, etiolated world of English letters. But it must be admitted that Campbell's experience and literary personality intersected rather obliquely with Baudelaire's: his brand of outsiderdom was that of the man of action, not the *flâneur* and explorer of dreamy narcotic landscapes. So while his own bright, hard-edged language is well adapted to Baudelaire's vehement moods ('To the Reader', 'Sympathetic Horror', 'Heautontimoroumenos'), even to his more vigorous ecstasies ('Elevation'), the more poised and reflective poetry is sometimes dealt with too brusquely: as David Wright observed in his 1961 British Council pamphlet on Campbell, 'it is as if the Parisian had been made to exchange his smoking-jacket and opium jar for cowboy leggings and a lariat'.[14] While this is something of an overstatement, Campbell's avowed aim 'to be as colloquial as possible' so as to keep faith with Baudelaire's 'horror of the pompously poetic' did sometimes lead him astray. Baudelaire is never pompous, but neither is his language colloquial; he often employs words and movements of an unpoetic register to telling effect, but always within the framework of a precise and formal discourse. Campbell's abrupt switches from a poetic and sometimes bizarrely archaic register, using words such as 'ruth' and 'thole', to a colloquial or simply prosaic one often lack such control. The rapidity of his work on the collection (he translated the whole of *Les Fleurs du Mal* and its associated pieces in a matter of months and once produced seventeen translations in a single night) may also help to explain its unevenness and occasional inaccuracy. Nevertheless there are, among a majority of serviceable translations, twenty or thirty very fine pieces and a few real gems of the translator's art.

Three years after the publication of Campbell's *Fleurs*, an anthology of similar scope to James Laver's Limited Editions Club volume appeared under the editorship of Jackson and Marthiel Mathews. This again covered the whole range of translations then published, rehabilitating Sturm (nineteen of whose poems Laver had unsuspectingly reproduced under the name of James Huneker, the editor of the pirated American edition) and reprinting many of Campbell's versions. It is particularly notable for the inclusion of three translations specially commissioned from the American poet Richard Wilbur. Wilbur follows in Millay's footsteps in his command of the leisured music of Baudelaire (compare their equally beautiful renderings of 'L'Invitation au Voyage'), and is the first postwar representative here of an urbane, cultured school of American poetry working a territory between classicism and symbolism, whose exponents can produce translations of an exceptional clarity. Anthony Hecht's four pieces and John Ashbery's translation of 'Paysage' exhibit similar virtues of metrical poise and vivid, nuanced vocabulary. All three respond sympathetically to Baudelaire's calmer moods, though Hecht also shows himself capable, in 'The Swan', of a steely rhetoric that transmits the passion of the original without slipping into stridency. Donald Justice's version of 'Les Metamorphoses du Vampire' is characterized by a similar firmness and control. Also of this period is Louise Varèse's unostentatiously faithful and intelligent complete translation of the prose poems. The nearest equivalents in Britain are Roy Fuller, who in his half-dozen Baudelaire versions combined fidelity to the text with a clipped, laconic diction recognizably his own, producing poems that say what Baudelaire meant them to say but which read with all the freshness and clarity of originals; and, for the prose poems, Michael Hamburger and Norman Cameron, both sensitive to nuance but capable too of fine flights of rhetoric.

Robert Lowell's versions, initially published in *Imitations* (1961) with other translations from classical and modern poetry, and reprinted by themselves in 1968 with expressionistic illustrations by Sidney Nolan, could hardly be more different from those of his compatriots just mentioned. His introduction to *Imitations* is by way of a self-justification and a disclaimer, marked by a slight disingenuousness. He explains the composition of such an assemblage of disparate originals by announcing that the book 'is partly self-sufficient and separate from its sources, and should be first read as a sequence, one voice running through many personalities': sources and personalities have been roped together as material for the expression of something beyond themselves, something of Lowell's own. Yet he presents himself, at least in the matter of technique, as an exponent of the middle way in translation: neither irresponsibly cavalier nor dogmatically attached to the precise sequence of the original, he dismisses 'strict metrical translators' as 'taxidermists, not poets', while castigating the 'sprawl of language, neither faithful nor distinguished' turned out by free verse translators. Again, he confesses (unwisely, in view of some of the criticism *Imitations* was to receive) to being 'reckless with literal meaning', but immediately counters that he has 'laboured hard to get the tone'. To the expected objection that the two factors might be in some way connected, he admits that 'Most often this has been *a* tone, for *the* tone is something that will always more or less escape transference to another language and cultural moment. I have tried hard to write live English and to do what my authors might have done if they were writing their poems now and in America.' In other words, he is offering not so much a translation of lines of verse as a transposition of attitudes and personalities into the modes of another culture. This, as noted above, was by no means a new conception: it is the basis of the great Augustan translations from classic sources; Pound, a key figure in Lowell's literary pantheon, had been reasserting its value for half a century; even Millay had given the possibility a passing nod in some of her Baudelaire translations. Lowell, however, tries to present himself as cutting through the tedious minutiae of literal translation in order to get at some sort of essence of the original, some *élan* of a creature observed on the wing, not in a glass case – only to confess in an aside that such a vital spirit is of course far too volatile to be caught, that in fact he has had to transplant a new, quite different spirit, but that he would rather the reader pretended that it was the original one so as to experience something equivalent, within the terms of modern culture, to what a contemporary of Baudelaire's might have experienced on reading the original poem.

Such an ambiguity of intentions could have proved fatal to his undertaking; but his actual method of translation is more single-minded than the introduction suggests. Of course his point about the transposition of historical and social context, and the impossibility of replicating the original context exactly in a present-day reader's mind, is valid and important. Translators of Baudelaire until then had either been unaware of the difficulty or had trusted to their readers' education and historical awareness to fill the gaps; or like Millay had projected their own urbane self-consciousness, born of their own time, tentatively out into a cosmopolitan literary space where it might link up with those aspects of Baudelaire's personality with which they felt a kinship. Now Lowell was by this stage in his career a poet whose myth of himself was at least as strong as Baudelaire's ever was – the same could be said of Millay to some extent, but as Mathews has observed, her own poetry was in a period of transition when she came to translate Baudelaire, and she treated his originals with a perhaps unexpected courtesy. Such accommodations were not for Lowell. Obviously in the very act of translating Baudelaire he was expressing a kinship with the French poet, with his suffering and with his mythically self-destructive trajectory; but, an insatiable raider of literary sources in his original work, in his translations he relived Baudelaire's rhetoric emphatically as his own. Sometimes this means that Baudelaire's words or structures serve merely as a framework for *poète maudit* Lowell's own melodramatic exclamations; but sometimes, while never ceasing to regard the original as workable source material ('a kind of quarry for his own poetry' in the words of the critic Burton Raffel)[15] rather than the mould into which his expression must be poured, he achieves a dramatic re-envisioning in modern terms of Baudelaire's actual intention – just the sort of deep mimesis at which he hints in his introduction. Lowell rarely reroutes his mode of expression to suit Baudelaire (and when he tries the result is usually flat), but when Baudelaire's vision coincides with Lowell's, as in the vertiginous terror of 'Le Gouffre', the result can be breathtakingly apt. Elsewhere we get pieces of Lowell tacked more or less convincingly on to a framework of Baudelaire, sometimes striking, often second-rate.

This maverick approach has won as many detractors as admirers. For many years after its publication, *Imitations* was the focus of fierce critical debate concerning the ethics of translation. Criticism has centred on two issues: whether Lowell's approach, as proclaimed in his introduction or enacted in his versions themselves, is artistically or even morally justifiable; and whether his work is actually technically competent considered in his own terms. Geoffrey Hill instigated the questioning of Lowell's motives, or the extent to which he succeeds in realizing them, with the observation that 'getting the tone' had become a matter of dramatizing the implicit meaning of the original, adding that such an approach 'is wholly valid, provided that the imitator knows precisely at what point he is becoming a dramatist!'[16].

Donald Carne-Ross has welcomed such transpositions as exemplifying our century's reinvention of the art of translation in terms of a process of interaction between two cultures, while insisting that most of Lowell's work does consist of genuine translations (inasmuch as they find valid equivalents for the tone of the original) rather than 'imitations' in the broad Augustan sense.[17] At the other extreme, John Simon expresses incredulity at the credulity of earlier critics, pointing out the howlers they have ignored or glossed over, and castigating Lowell's persistent distortion of tone as a self-centred and immoral betrayal of his originals.[18] Simon concludes that Lowell is Pound's inadequate imitator, lacking his master's ability to 'ignore his original . . . sublimely'. Lowell, though, was not consciously aiming to transcend his original, though there are certainly many lines at which he has glanced before producing a fluent but unmeaningful misreading. His versions are careless and egocentric, but they succeed where they do almost because of this: the prevailing roughness throws into relief the sudden accesses of intense subjective sympathy.

Lowell's approach to translation has been considered in some detail because the issues it raises are increasingly relevant to recent translations of Baudelaire. From the 1960s onward 'straight' versions of his poems begin to give place to freer and more radical approaches. His creative and personal identity and the cultural meaning of his work are taken more and more as given – a consensus is assumed to exist which can serve as a point of departure: the poem to be translated becomes a found object to be distorted at will or to serve as the armature for a new work; or it is a text to be treated ironically, and redirected by internal references to Baudelaire's life or other writings. Such procedures could be seen as the controlled and self-conscious descendants of Symons's desperate improvisations, but in general these later imaginative translators are not content simply to lash Baudelaire to the careering wagon of their own obsessions: even their most extreme reworkings tend to be directed at a genuine elucidation of his oeuvre or a genuinely enriching link

between his preoccupations and their own. Whereas Campbell
expressed such an impulse by working Baudelairean imagery into
entirely new poems, there has more recently been a tendency to
recontextualize the original verse without breaking up its structure. So
Seamus Heaney turns in *North* (1975) to 'Le Squelette Laboureur' as a
suitable scheme of imagery to evoke the mute persistence, the universal-
ity of the torments endured by those Bronze Age sacrificial victims
about whose preserved corpses he writes, and to echo that strange blend
of intimacy and unbridgeable distance with which he considers them.
The few details he adds particularize the poem just enough to enable
it to fit into his own imaginative discourse; the result, far from being a
betrayal of Baudelaire's original, is an extension of its domain: the
fraternal probity and seriousness of Heaney's use of the poem open a
window through which Baudelaire's signification can operate in terri-
tory unknown to him in his lifetime. As an equally responsible translator
of Baudelaire, Vernon Watkins, observed in his essay 'The Translation
of Poetry', the addition of material does not matter 'if it is something
essential to the fulfilment of the translated poem, something [the poet]
himself would have chosen'[19] were he situated within the translator's
historical context. A more extreme approach is illustrated by Nicholas
Moore's extraordinary multiple translation of 'Je suis comme le roi . . .'
which keeps more or less to the structure of the original but imports a
welter of inescapably modern and seedily English imagery, exploiting
the claustrophobic atmosphere of the 'Spleen' poems as material for his
own private mythologies.

  Over the last two decades, several poets have turned their attention
to the question of how to render in modern terms those ecstatic and
decadent aspects of Baudelaire's poetic personality that so attracted some
of his earlier translators. Some have sought to achieve his proto-symbolist
élan through metrical means, either through free verse (as in James
Liddy's collection *Baudelaire's Bar Flowers*, 1975, which situates the
poetry in a dreamy, erotically charged West Coast milieu) or prosodic
complexity (for example Ciaran Carson's 'Correspondances', 1993,
with its long rhythmical lines suggestive of trance). Such experiments
may be successful on their own terms, but free verse in particular

inevitably discards the nuances and rhetorical emphases of Baudelaire's balanced and subtly patterned prosody.

A more thoughtful and generally more successful approach is offered by Richard Howard in his unrhymed metrical translation of *Les Fleurs du Mal* (1982).[20] In his Foreword, Howard justifies at some length his decision to eschew rhyme without explaining exactly why he has done so, though his motivation was clearly to avoid the enormous constraint involved in finding equivalent rhymes through an entire collection, which as we have seen has doomed even the strongest of rhyming complete translations or large selections to its share of unsatisfactory versions. What he does assert is his confidence in the alternative means he has employed 'to make up for, even to suggest, the consentaneous regularities that the persistent use of rhyme affords' and to seek out the 'secret architecture' of Baudelaire's poetry. In practice this involves a reliance on careful stress-patterning and a sophisticated use of alliteration and near-alliteration, which is often surprisingly successful in capturing the tone of the original, especially in Baudelaire's more intimate or nostalgic moods – the 'private register' which Howard admits in his Foreword to having particularly striven for and which he presents with great lucidity. If he is sometimes less successful when dealing with the more violently cynical outbursts, this may result less from any linguistic or prosodic failure than from an avowed reluctance on his part to engage too closely with 'the splendour and misery of cities, of bodies . . . that vast background of negativity against which finally rises the success of *Les Fleurs du Mal*'. He is a little uncomfortable with the darker aspects of Baudelaire's persona, and this uncertainty underlies his goal of 'articulating a sustained structure among all the poems' rather than varnishing the surface of every piece (again he is quite frank about this, admitting that 'If I could not always love my originals, I have endeavoured to serve them by an attempt to leave them alone . . . Wanting to keep Baudelaire, I wanted to keep him at a certain distance' – in contrast to the very personal engagements of certain other translators). This approach has resulted in the most consistently faithful complete translation yet produced, and one much less remote and disengaged than some of his pronouncements might suggest. It is a rather cool and classical reading of Baudelaire, but none the less rich in music and by no means devoid of passion, as his fine version of 'Un Voyage à Cythère' shows.

A strong contrast to Howard's clarity and detachment is afforded by the most striking of all the recent brushes with the bohemian side of Baudelaire: the growing body of translations, now about fifteen in all, by Jeremy Reed, published during the last few years over several volumes of his original poetry. Reed, a Francophile and something of a latter-day bohemian, whose ventures into fiction have included novels based on the lives of Sade and Lautréamont, identifies strongly with Baudelaire – as witness a striking sequence of verse monologues in his collection *Nero* (1985), in which he assumes the voice of the poet in middle age, reflecting on his formative influences (his mother, the journey to Mauritius, Jeanne Duval) in imagery which borrows heavily from *Les Fleurs du Mal*. But in many of his actual translations he has appeared, by his choice of original and by the manner of his treatment, to press-gang Baudelaire into his own crusade to reclaim the frankly erotic as a fit subject for serious poetry. This need not be a bad thing – the erotic aspects of Baudelaire's oeuvre have had a raw deal from translators over the last century and a quarter, and Reed might have been expected to be a good person to set the record straight. Often, however, he tries too hard to find a contemporary voice, awkwardly updating Baudelaire with modern phrases and images that manage to hit the wrong note, like an adult trying to converse in the argot of teenagers. From time to time he succeeds in imparting an authentic intensity, but many of these versions are frankly not as convincing as the best of his original poetry in the same vein. This is a pity, for he is a poet vividly responsive to the textures of urban life, and his imagery, voluptuous or crystalline, has quite a kinship to Baudelaire's. It will be interesting to see whether he decides to apply himself to other areas of the French poet's territory, in particular the rest of the 'Tableaux Parisiens' (from which he has so far produced four powerful, if uneven, translations) and the poems of alienation or metaphysical anguish, which he has not yet addressed at all.

In the meantime, Peter Dale, Dick Davis and Alistair Elliot, among others, continue to produce thoughtful and direct versions, keeping mainly to the familiar territory of shorter lyrics from 'Spleen et Idéal' ('Harmonie du Soir', 'Parfum Exotique', 'Correspondances',

'L'Albatros' and others of that order will always continue to attract most of the attention) but producing the occasional surprise. Dale has translated a broad selection, not yet collected into single volume; and Davis has the makings of another Roy Fuller in his firm, lucid handling of Baudelaire's parabolic mode – comparing his fine version of 'La Rançon' to Fuller's of 'Les Hiboux', one has the same sense of the lyric having arrived on the page fully formed, perfectly poised and simple.

A survey of these most recent translations may give the impression that Baudelaire has become such a familiar feature of the modern literary landscape that to translate him or invoke his imagery or personality in original poetry no longer indicates (*pace* Reed) the adoption of any particular aesthetic stance, but is no more than a matter of individual preference, an occasion for the exercise of poetic craftsmanship. Certainly his urban imagery – by virtue of the enormous influence it has exerted, directly and indirectly, upon the course of modern poetry – has lost something of its inspiring sense of danger, although paradoxically the very familiarity to present-day eyes of the territory it inhabits may help us to a sense of kinship with its author. More specifically, Baudelaire's visions of intoxication, decadence and degradation have been outdone in extremism by much that has been written in the last half-century, though again the unrivalled clarity of his dispatches from the precipice of alienation will ensure their truth and relevance for generations to come. His poems of the relations between men and women, on the other hand, explore attitudes and conceptions some of which have been to a large extent expunged from our everyday, not to mention our poetic, discourse. The literary orthodoxy of our own time militates against the frank investigation of sexual motivation almost as much as did that of Baudelaire's day, albeit from different motives: the revolution in sexual mores of the intervening century and a quarter has, paradoxically, multiplied the danger which he himself indignantly denounced when the first edition of *Les Fleurs* was seized – that of being read in part only, of being more or less wilfully misunderstood by the hunters of convenient scapegoats. The language of sexual submissiveness and idolatry so central to Baudelaire's self-definition may now appear quaint or ridiculous unless presented ironically or (as with Reed) in a context of conventionalized fetishism and sado-masochism; yet the language of sexualized violence through which he mediated his nihilism and impotence, and which now risks proscription as a glorification of rape and homicide, remains in truth a fundamentally metaphorical means of expressing and analysing certain real states of mind and relations between society and the individual, concerning which we have hardly yet attained a full understanding. Regrettably, but unsurprisingly, this strand of his output has (with the exception of Reed's versions) been little translated of late.

What of Baudelaire, then, is left still raw and unassimilated to offer inspiration to future generations of English-language poets, and what directions can we expect future translations of his work to take? There is undoubtedly a scope and a need for further evaluation in English of the more personal aspects of that 'whole lower register' of which Jackson Mathews hailed Shanks as the first true champion: Baudelaire's darkest work still has an important contribution to make to our poetic understanding of sexual psychology and social alienation, if there are translators prepared for the difficult and perhaps thankless task of transmitting his anatomies of evil and indifference in all their terrible lucidity. The more general urban matter, the sense of the often inspiriting and serendipitous complexity of the city, will remain a source of inspiration to poets of modern life, even if the full strength of its revolutionary impact has long been assimilated. But while Baudelaire's identity as an icon of the Modern has faded, it may be that his pronouncements on the roles of the poet and of art in general (in particular the visual arts) are set to become the focus of renewed interest. We have almost lost the habit – perhaps since the backlash set in against Lowell's generation – of casting the poet in the role of heroic outcast: even the persona of the artist as counter-cultural revolutionary has worn badly in the English-speaking world. Yet in the cultural context of today, where the innovative artist, unless commercially successful, courts journalistic derision and political hostility, Baudelaire's cynicism, his heroically doomed persona, his sympathy for the underclass and his insistence on the divine if fallen nature of human creativity are as relevant as at any time since his death. If certain of these considerations are not felt to lend themselves as readily to original poetry as they once did, they can yet be approached anew through the prism of translation and adaptation – as some of Reed's versions, and Davis's, suggest, like Lowell's and Campbell's before them. Aided by this continual reassessment and renewal, Baudelaire's work will remain an active presence in contemporary letters, and a source of strength and inspiration to the poets and readers of our time and time to come.

Notes

1. Jules Laforgue, 'Notes sur Baudelaire', in *Mélanges posthumes*, Paris, 1903.
2. Aleister Crowley, *Little Poems in Prose*, Paris, 1928, Preface.
3. Lewis Piaget Shanks, *Baudelaire: Flesh and Spirit*, Boston, 1930, Preface.
4. *Les Fleurs du Mal*, LXXXI.
5. *Charles Baudelaire: Intimate Journals*, translated by Christopher Isherwood, with an introduction by W. H. Auden, Hollywood, 1947, and London, 1949.
6. The review, submitted to *Le Pays*, was refused on the grounds that Baudelaire's case was *sub judice*. It was one of the 'articles justificatifs' printed with the 1861 edition of *Les Fleurs du Mal* and is reproduced in the Crépet-Blin-Pichois edition, Paris, Vol. I, 1968.
7. Algernon Charles Swinburne, 'Les Fleurs du Mal', collected in *Les Fleurs du Mal and Other Studies*, London, 1913.
8. Arthur Symons, 'Charles Baudelaire', *English Review* XXVI, 1918; 'A Study of Charles Baudelaire', *London Quarterly Review* CXXX, 1918; *Charles Baudelaire: A Study*, London, 1920.
9. T. S. Eliot, 'Poet and Saint', *Dial* LXXXII, 1927.
10. J. Mathews, 'Baudelaire in English', *Sewanee Review* LVII, 1949.
11. T. S. Eliot, 'Baudelaire': prefatory essay to Isherwood's translation of the *Intimate Journals*, London, 1930.
12. T. S. Eliot, 'What Dante Means to Me', *Adelphi* XXVII, 1951.
13. George Steiner, 'From Poet to Poet', *Sunday Times*, London, 6 October 1968.
14. David Wright, *Roy Campbell* (Writers and Their Work, 137), London, 1961.
15. Burton Raffel, 'Robert Lowell's *Imitations*', *Translation Review* V, 1980.
16. Geoffrey Hill, 'Robert Lowell: Contrasts and Repetitions', *Essays in Criticism* XIII, 1963.
17. Donald Carne-Ross, 'The Two Voices of Translation', in T. Parkinson, *Robert Lowell: A Collection of Critical Essays*, 1968.

18. John Simon, 'Abuse of Privilege: Lowell as Translator', *Hudson Review* XX, 1967.

19. Vernon Watkins, 'The Translation of Poetry', in his *Selected Verse Translations*, London, 1977.

20. Richard Howard, *Charles Baudelaire: Les Fleurs du Mal*, 1982, Foreword. Howard's translation was republished in 1993 by Everyman, London, but without the Foreword.

LES FLEURS DU MAL

ROY CAMPBELL (1901–57)

South African poet and translator, Roy Campbell was born in Durban of Scottish descent. He left for England at seventeen to study for admission to Oxford, but changed his mind and plunged into the literary world which he would court, scandalize and lampoon for the rest of his life. After spells in South Africa and Provence, reflected, along with his reading of Baudelaire and the French Symbolists, in the intense but formal lyrics of *Adamastor* (1930) and *Flowering Reeds* (1933), trailing feuds and tales of physical prowess, he moved with his wife to Spain, a country whose harsh contrasts and traditionalism suited his temperament, and became a Roman Catholic. He made no secret of his Nationalist sympathies, and after being wounded while reporting on the Madrid front for the *Tablet*, outraged the British liberal establishment with *Flowering Rifle* (1939), a lengthy paean to General Franco which poured scorn on the Republican cause. After serving in East Africa in the Second World War, he settled in London and resumed with gusto and occasional fisticuffs his feuds with the left-wing poetic establishment; in 1952 he moved to Portugal and for the rest of his life was increasingly involved in translation. His death in a car crash silenced a talent by no means exhausted.

For all the extravagance of his life and occasional garrulity of his original work, he was a serious-minded and versatile translator, tackling poets very diverse in character, and communicating the mordancy of Horace, the vertigo of Rimbaud, the directness of Lorca with honesty and a degree of self-effacement. At his best he was able to channel the passion and fertility of his own poetic language into a wholly convincing mediation of another writer's vision – nowhere more so than in his celebrated *Poems of St John of the Cross* (1951), which T. S. Eliot considered to be unmatchable. His complete translation of *Les Fleurs du Mal* (1952), though less consistently brilliant, scores many notable successes.

Here, 'weeping tears he cannot smother' is a seriously inaccurate translation of '*l'œil chargé d'un pleur involontaire*', but otherwise the mood

of this liminary poem is well caught, particularly the hyper-romanticism
of stanzas six, seven and eight.

To the Reader

Folly and error, avarice and vice,
Employ our souls and waste our bodies' force.
As mangey beggars incubate their lice,
We nourish our innocuous remorse.

Our sins are stubborn, craven our repentance.
For our weak vows we ask excessive prices.
Trusting our tears will wash away the sentence,
We sneak off where the muddy road entices.

Cradled in evil, that Thrice-Great Magician,
10 The Devil, rocks our souls, that can't resist;
And the rich metal of our own volition
Is vaporised by that sage alchemist.

The Devil pulls the strings by which we're worked:
By all revolting objects lured, we slink
Hellwards; each day down one more step we're jerked
Feeling no horror, through the shades that stink.

Just as a lustful pauper bites and kisses
The scarred and shrivelled breast of an old whore,
We steal, along the roadside, furtive blisses,
20 Squeezing them, like stale oranges, for more.

Packed tight, like hives of maggots, thickly seething,
Within our brains a host of demons surges.
Deep down into our lungs at every breathing,
Death flows, an unseen river, moaning dirges.

If rape or arson, poison, or the knife
Has wove no pleasing patterns in the stuff
Of this drab canvas we accept as live –
It is because we are not bold enough!

Amongst the jackals, leopards, mongrels, apes,
30 Snakes, scorpions, vultures, that with hellish din,
Squeal, roar, writhe, gambol, crawl, with monstrous shapes,
In each man's foul menagerie of sin –

There's one more damned than all. He never gambols,
Nor crawls, nor roars, but, from the rest withdrawn,
Gladly of this whole earth would make a shambles
And swallow up existence with a yawn . . .

Boredom! He smokes his hookah, while he dreams
Of gibbets, weeping tears he cannot smother.
You know this dainty monster, too, it seems –
40 Hypocrite reader! – You! – My twin! – My brother!

(1952)

Spleen et Idéal

(Spleen and the Ideal)

PHILIP HIGSON (1933–) and E. R. ASHE (1932–)

Higson and Ashe produced a complete verse translation of *Les Fleurs du Mal* in 1975 which was reprinted by the Limouse Press in 1992. Higson has also published *Limouse Nudes inspired by Baudelaire* (1994) and, in 1986, a translation of Maurice Rollinat's *Les Névroses*. His and Ashe's translations are accurate but not always inspired. The rather Victorian diction of this poem does, however, mirror to some extent that of the original.

Benediction   I

When, by divine authority's decree,
The Poet in this woeful world appears,
His outraged mother, moved to blasphemy,
Raises her fists at God, who pitying hears:

'Ah! would that I a viper's brood had bred,
Rather than grant this creature nourishment!
I curse that night of pleasures swiftly fled
For which my womb conceived this punishment!

Since, of all womankind, you now desire
That I should earn my husband's contumely,
And since I cannot toss into the fire,
Like some old love-note, this monstrosity,

Then shall I turn the spite you vent on me
Upon this tool of your malignant power,
And twist so thoroughly this stunted tree
That its infected buds shall never flower!'

And thus she swallows down her slavering bile.
But, failing Heaven's designs to understand,
Herself, deep down in Hell, begins to pile
20   The pyres that for maternal crimes are planned.

Yet neath an Angel's unseen guardianship,
In sunlight sports that infant pariah
Who, in whatever he may taste or sip,
Finds rosy nectar and ambrosia.

He talks with clouds and with the winds he plays,
And sings of Calvary, to rapture stirred;
The Spirit following in this pilgrim's ways
Now weeps to see him blithe as any bird.

Those he would love watch him with fearful eye,
30   Or, heartened by his sweet tranquillity,
To see who first can wring from him a cry,
Upon him prove their sly ferocity.

Into the bread and wine laid for his use
Foul ashes mixed with sputum vile they aim;
And that he touched these hypocrites traduce,
And, with resembling him, each other blame.

His wife proclaims in every public place:
'Because my charms his adoration hold,
For him the ancient idols I'll replace,
40   And like them have my body decked with gold.

And I shall glut myself with myrrh and nard,
Sweet incense, genuflexions, meats and wine,
And, from that soul that holds me in regard,
Shall, laughing, steal the homages divine!

When of these impious mockeries I tire,
My frail yet powerful hand I'll on him lay,
My nails, as sharp as those of harpies dire,
Straight to his heart shall single out the way.

And, like a throbbing fledgling, from his breast
50 I'll wrench that crimson heart out bodily,
And as a morsel for my favourite beast
I'll cast it on the ground disdainfully!'

To Heaven, where a rich throne greets his gaze,
The Poet lifts his pious arms, serene;
His lucid spirit's penetrating rays
Distract him from the nation's seething spleen.

'Bless you, O God, who sent us torment here
To cleanse us of our rank iniquities,
As the most pure, most potent elixir
60 Prepares the strong for sacred ecstasies!

I know that for the Poet you, at least,
Reserve a place in heavenly Companies,
That you invite him to the timeless feast
Of Thrones, of Virtues, and of Sovereignties;

I know that suffering brings nobility
Which powers of earth and hell cannot debase;
And that my mystic crown must fashioned be
Of treasures drawn from every age and place.

But old Palmyra's vanished gems past price,
70 Pearls of the seas, and metals yet unseen,
Though set by your own hand, would not suffice
For that great diadem's clear and dazzling sheen.

For it shall be of purest lucency,
From out the source of rays primaeval drawn,
Beside which mortal eyes' resplendency
Is that of mirrors tarnished and forlorn!'

(1972)

RICHARD WILBUR (1921–   )

Poet and academic, Wilbur was educated at Amherst and Harvard. His long and distinguished poetic career has won him many honours, including two Pulitzer Prizes (1957, 1989) and a term as US Poet Laureate (1987–8). He has been an acclaimed translator of Molière and Racine, and adapted an opera from Voltaire's *Candide*. His three translations from Baudelaire (all written for Marthiel and Jackson Mathews's 1955 anthology) shun the poet's darker and more difficult imaginings, and indeed include two of his purest evocations of sensual delight: but Wilbur's tactful, poised and beautiful realizations suggest that he chose with care originals perfectly attuned to his temperament and powers.

'L'Albatros' probably owes its status as an anthology piece to its final, explanatory stanza, which was not added until some time after the composition of the previous three. (A 1970s biography is even called *Baudelaire, Prince of Clouds*). It has often been translated, in a variety of styles; for example, the slang word *brûle-gueule* (old pipe) in line 11 tempted Kingsley Amis to translate the whole piece into Cockney. Wilbur strikes a balance between occasionally prosaic diction and high Romantic vision.

The Albatross   II

Often, for pastime, mariners will ensnare
The albatross, that vast sea-bird who sweeps
On high companionable pinion where
Their vessel glides upon the bitter deeps.

Torn from his native space, this captive king
Flounders upon the deck in stricken pride,
And pitiably lets his great white wing
Drag like a heavy paddle at his side.

This rider of winds, how awkward he is, and weak!
How droll he seems, who was all grace of late!
A sailor pokes a pipestem into his beak,
Another, hobbling, mocks his trammeled gait.

The Poet is like this monarch of the clouds,
Familiar of storms, of stars, and of all high things;
Exiled on earth amidst its hooting crowds,
He cannot walk, borne down by giant wings.

(1955)

ROY CAMPBELL

Elevation   III

Above the valleys and the lakes: beyond
The woods, seas, clouds and mountain-ranges: far
Above the sun, the aethers silver-swanned
With nebulae, and the remotest star,

My spirit! with agility you move
Like a strong swimmer with the seas to fight,
Through the blue vastness furrowing your groove
With an ineffable and male delight.

Far from these foetid marshes, be made pure
10   In the pure air of the superior sky,
And drink, like some most exquisite liqueur,
The fire that fills the lucid realms on high.

Beyond where cares or boredom hold dominion,
Which charge our fogged existence with their spleen,
Happy is he who with a stalwart pinion
Can seek those fields so shining and serene:

Whose thoughts, like larks, rise on the freshening breeze,
Who fans the morning with his tameless wings,
Skims over life, and understands with ease
20   The speech of flowers and other voiceless things.

(1952)

Correspondances

'Correspondances', like Rimbaud's 'Voyelles', comes to the twentieth-century reader laden with programmatic significance it was not designed to bear. Rather than prefiguring Symbolism, this poem echoes Romantic ideas. The comparison of a temple interior to a forest recalls a famous passage in Chateaubriand, while the doctrine of 'correspondences' between the spiritual and material worlds goes back to Swedenborg. Baudelaire acknowledges this filiation in the second part of his essay on Victor Hugo written for the *Revue fantaisiste* in 1861, when he speaks of the poet's power to transmit and interpret the 'sensations morales' which come to us from '*la nature inanimée, ou dite inanimée*'.

It is perhaps the first tercet, with its (for the time) daringly synaesthetic comparisons, that has drawn so many translators to attempt versions.

Correspondances   IV

> La Nature est un temple où de vivants piliers
> Laissent parfois sortir de confuses paroles;
> L'homme y passe à travers des forêts de symboles
> Qui l'observent avec des regards familiers.
>
> Comme de longs échos qui de loin se confondent
> Dans une ténébreuse et profonde unité,
> Vaste comme la nuit et comme la clarté,
> Les parfums, les couleurs et les sons se répondent.
>
> Il est des parfums frais comme des chairs d'enfants,
> Doux comme les hautbois, verts comme les prairies,
> – Et d'autres, corrompus, riches et triomphants,
>
> Ayant l'expansion des choses infinies,
> Comme l'ambre, le musc, le benjoin et l'encens,
> Qui chantent les transports de l'esprit et des sens.

FRANCES CORNFORD (1886–1960)

A granddaughter of Charles Darwin and related on her mother's side to William Wordsworth, Frances Cornford spent most of her life in Cambridge, where she married the Classical scholar Francis Cornford: their eldest child was the poet John Cornford, killed in the Spanish Civil War. She began to write poetry at sixteen, publishing her first collection in 1910; she was a close friend of Rupert Brooke, who gave her much encouragement. In 1959 she was awarded the Queen's Gold Medal for Poetry. Her published translations include a volume of Russian poetry and a selection from Louis Aragon.

Correspondences   IV

In Nature's temple living columns rise
Whence issue, sometimes, words confusedly,
Man threads a wood of symbols. Every tree
Watches him passing by with intimate eyes.

As to our ears long far-off echoes reach
Merged in a deep and sombre unity,
Vast as the night and morning's clarity,
So scents, sounds, colours answer each to each.

Some scents are cool like children's flesh, some shed
10   An hautboy's sweetness, some are green as spring,
– Others corrupt and rich triumphing,

And these, like infinite things, have power to spread,
As amber, musk and myrrh and frankincense
Which chant the spirit's marriage with the sense.

(1976)

ALLEN TATE (1899–1979)

Tate was educated at Vanderbilt University. Nineteenth-century French poetry was an important early influence on his writing, but there are very few translations among his published works. This is one of only two versions of Baudelaire, both dating from 1924.

Correspondences   IV

All nature is a temple where the alive
Pillars breathe often a tremor of mixed words;
Man wanders in a forest of accords
That peer familiarly from each ogive.

Like thinning echoes tumbling to sleep beyond
In a unity umbrageous and infinite,
Vast as the night stupendously moonlit,
All smells and colors and sounds correspond.

Odors blown sweet as infants' naked flesh,
Soft as oboes, green as a studded plain,
– Others, corrupt, rich and triumphant, thresh

Expansions to the infinite of pain:
Amber and myrrh, benzoin and musk condense
To transports of the spirit and the sense!

(1924)

ROY CAMPBELL

Correspondences   IV

Nature's a temple where each living column,
At times, gives forth vague words. There Man advances
Through forest-groves of symbols, strange and solemn,
Who follow him with their familiar glances.

As long-drawn echoes mingle and transfuse
Till in a deep, dark unison they swoon,
Vast as the night or as the vault of noon –
So are commingled perfumes, sounds, and hues.

There can be perfumes cool as children's flesh,
Like fiddles, sweet, like meadows greenly fresh.
Rich, complex, and triumphant, others roll

With the vast range of all non-finite things –
Amber, musk, incense, benjamin, each sings
The transports of the senses and the soul.

(1952)

RICHARD WILBUR

Correspondences   IV

Nature is a temple whose living colonnades
Breathe forth a mystic speech in fitful sighs;
Man wanders among symbols in those glades
Where all things watch him with familiar eyes.

Like dwindling echoes gathered far away
Into a deep and thronging unison
Huge as the night or as the light of day,
All scents and sounds and colors meet as one.

Perfumes there are as sweet as the oboe's sound,
Green as the prairies, fresh as a child's caress,
– And there are others, rich, corrupt, profound

And of an infinite pervasiveness,
Like myrrh, or musk, or amber, that excite
The ecstasies of sense, the soul's delight.

(1955)

CIARAN CARSON (1948–)

Carson was born in Belfast and educated at Queen's University; he now works for the Arts Council of Northern Ireland. He has published several collections of verse, winning a Gregory Award for the first, *New Estates* (1976). 'Correspondences' is taken from *First Language* (1993), which also contains several translations from Ovid and a version of Rimbaud's 'Le Bateau Ivre'.

Correspondances   IV

Nature is a Temple: its colonnaded trunks blurt out, from time
　　to time, a verdurous babble;
The dark symbolic forest eyes you with familiarity, from the
　　verge of Parable.

Self-confounding echoes buzz and mingle through the gloomy
　　arbours;
Vowels, perfumes, stars swarm in like fireflies from the
　　midnight blue of harbours.

The quartet yawns and growls at you with amber, rosin,
　　incense, musk;
Horsehair on the catgut is ecstatic with its soul and spirit
　　music –

Prairie greens, the *oms* and *ahs* of oboes, soft as the bloom on
　　infant
Baby-skin; and other great hits, smothered in the triumph of
　　the infinite.

(1993)

EDNA ST VINCENT MILLAY
(1892–1950)

Millay was educated at Vassar College. Her *A Few Figs from Thistles* (1920) won her a reputation both as a poet and as a mouthpiece for independent modern womanhood, and helped her to a Pulitzer Prize two years later – the first to be awarded to a woman poet. Her wry, worldly-wise poetic persona made her something of a romantic icon for her contemporaries – Dorothy Parker is among those to have attested to her influence.

Initially invited by George Dillon to contribute an introduction to his translations of Baudelaire, she relates enthusiastically how she finished by producing half the collection herself. Her fluent translations speak as often as not in her own relaxed, informal voice, so that one can easily take for granted their considerable sensitivity to the imagery of the original in the illusion that one is simply reading an original poem. Taken as a whole, they amply justify her audacity in playing the cuckoo in Dillon's nest.

Baudelaire's final image is of a '*saltimbanque à jeun*, [*étalant*] *tes appas*', a street-acrobat who has not eaten that day, showing off her (physical) charms. There is no suggestion that the acrobat is naked, nor would contemporary decorum have allowed it. Millay fudges the suggestion of sexual display, while Howard exaggerates it.

The Mercenary Muse   VIII

Muse of my heart, so fond of palaces, reply:
When January sends those blizzards wild and white,
Shall you have any fire at all to huddle by,
Chafing your violet feet in the black snowy night?

Think: when the moon shines through the window, shall you
      try
To thaw your marble shoulders in her square of light?
Think: when your purse is empty and your palate dry,
Can you from the starred heaven snatch all the gold in sight?

No, no; if you would earn your bread, you have no choice
10   But to become a choir-boy, and chant in a loud voice
Te Deums you have no faith in, and swing your censer high;

Or be a mountebank, employing all your art –
Yes, on an empty stomach and with an anguished heart –
To chase the boredom of the liverish gallery.

(1936)

RICHARD HOWARD (1929–   )

Howard, American poet and translator, studied at Columbia and the
Sorbonne. He won a Pulitzer Prize in 1969 for his third collection
Untitled Subjects. Misgivings (1979) consists of a series of imagined
responses on the part of various historical subjects to their portraits by
Baudelaire's friend, the photographer Nadar. Howard is a distinguished
and extremely prolific translator of French prose, in particular of the
works of Roland Barthes, André Gide and various exponents of the
nouveau roman. His decision (admittedly eloquently justified – see Intro-

duction) to translate the whole of *Les Fleurs du Mal* into blank verse
inevitably deprives his versions of some of the music of the originals,
and is especially problematic in the sonnets, where argument, form
and rhyme are intimately linked. Nevertheless, his freedom from the
constraint of rhyme has permitted him to produce translations often of
considerable subtlety and acuity.

The Muse for Hire   VIII

My palace-loving Muse, can you afford –
once January launches out of the North
night after night of desolating snow –
the coals to comfort your frostbitten feet?

Are streetlamps through your shutters stove enough
to make your huddled shoulders warm again?
When your belly is as empty as your purse,
what will you do – harvest the stars for gold?

Try other ways to earn your nightly bread:
suppose you swing a censer (just for show)
and like a choirboy mumble all the hymns;

or, naked as an acrobat, reveal
laughing charms so wet with secret tears
they rouse the tired businessman to pay.

(1982)

MICHAEL VINCE (1947–   )

Vince lived in Greece for seventeen years as a teacher of English and has published two collections of English poetry.

The Enemy   X

My childhood days were dark with stormy weather
And rarely bursts of sunlight pierced the rain;
Such havoc came from wind and hail together
That in my garden few ripe fruits remain.

Here in the autumn of my thoughts I stand,
And I must set to work with rake and spade
To put to rights the sodden plots of land,
The holes the size of tombs the rain has made.

Who knows if the new flowers of which I dream
Will find in earth so washed by such a stream
The food they need to strengthen every part?

Oh grief on grief! Time feeds upon our lives,
The hidden Enemy gnaws us at the heart,
And from the blood we lose it grows and thrives.

(1997)

GEORGE DILLON (1906–68)

Dillon studied at the University of Chicago. His first collection of poetry, *Boy in the Wind*, was published in 1927. He worked as an advertising copywriter until he won a Pulitzer Prize for his second collection *The Flowering Stone* (1931), whereupon he spent two years in Paris and began work on his translations of Baudelaire. These were published in 1935 along with those by Edna St Vincent Millay.

The quatrains of the original sonnet, 'Le Guignon', are closely based on Longfellow's 'A Psalm of Life' (1839), and the tercets on Gray's 'Elegy Written in a Country Churchyard' ('Full many a gem of purest ray serene', etc.)

Ill-starred   XI

A man would needs be brave and strong
As Sisyphus, for such a task!
It is not greater zeal I ask –
But life is brief, and art is long.

To a forsaken mound of clay
Where no admirers ever come,
My heart, like an invisible drum,
Goes beating a dead march all day.

Many a jewel of untold worth
10   Lies slumbering at the core of earth,
In darkness and oblivion drowned;

Many a flower has bloomed and spent
The secret of its passionate scent
Upon the wilderness profound.

(1936)

RICHARD HOWARD

Howard's version is more knowing. 'Hippocrates remarked' and 'the poet mourns' draw the reader's attention to the intertextuality of the piece. 'Forgotten in the dust' is a poor substitute for 'the dark unfathom'd caves of Ocean', however; Baudelaire had '*sondes*', plumb-lines.

Artist Unknown   XI

Flesh is willing, but the Soul requires
    Sisyphean patience for its song.
Time, Hippocrates remarked, is short
        and Art is long.

No illustrious tombstones ornament
    the lonely churchyard where I often go
to hear my heart, a muffled drum, parade
        incognito.

'Many a gem,' the poet mourns, abides
10   forgotten in the dust,
        unnoticed there;

'many a rose' regretfully confides
    the secret of its scent
        to empty air.

(1982)

F. P. STURM (1879–1942)

Sturm studied medicine at Aberdeen University, where he began to contribute poems and articles to periodicals. He met W. B. Yeats about 1903, probably in consequence of their shared interest in esoteric philosophy: they corresponded about poetry and spiritual matters for many years. Thomas Sturge Moore (see below, p. 129) was another influence; it was he who designed the cover of Sturm's last published work, *Eternal Helen*.

Sturm's first volume of verse was published in 1905 and sold so poorly that he was obliged to defray the publisher's losses. Nevertheless he was commissioned soon after to translate a selection of Baudelaire for the Canterbury Poets Series. This too appears to have made little impression at its first, British, publication in 1906: however, a pirated edition appeared in New York in 1919 and a version of it (with translations by other poets) remained in print through succeeding impressions for some years thereafter. These editions did not even carry Sturm's name – a circumstance that led James Laver to reproduce poems from them as by James Huneker, the 1919 edition's (named) editor and assumed author. Meanwhile Arthur Symons's translations of Baudelaire had been accepted by British readers as authoritative, and Sturm had withdrawn from literature altogether to pursue his private spiritual investigations and his distinguished career as an ear, nose and throat specialist, though he continued to correspond with Yeats. In an article of 1949 Jackson Mathews drew attention to the high quality of Sturm's translations, on which he drew heavily for the anthology which he published with Marthiel Mathews in 1955.

A Former Life   XII

> Long since, I lived beneath vast porticoes,
> By many ocean-sunsets tinged and fired,
> Where mighty pillars, in majestic rows,
> Seemed like basaltic caves when day expired.

The rolling surge that mirrored all the skies
Mingled its music, turbulent and rich,
Solemn and mystic, with the colours which
The setting sun reflected in my eyes.

And there I lived amid voluptuous calms,
10   In splendours of blue sky and wandering wave,
Tended by many a naked, perfumed slave,

Who fanned my languid brow with waving palms.
They were my slaves – the only care they had
To know what secret grief had made me sad.

(1906)

RICHARD HOWARD

Gypsies on the Road   XIII

The prophet-tribe with burning eyes set out
yesterday, women bearing on their backs
brats whose clamorous greed is satisfied
by offering an ever-ready dug;

beside a wagon sheltering their brood
the men trudge, shouldering their oily guns
and gazing nowhere, eyelids heavier
for having lost their castles in the air.

The cricket hidden in its sandy lair
10   sings all the louder as they pass;
a favoring Goddess makes the desert bloom,

and where they wander springs transform the rock,
these vagabonds in front of whom unfurl
familiar empires of oncoming night.

(1982)

JAMES ELROY FLECKER
(1884–1915)

Flecker developed an interest in French poetry while at Trinity College, Oxford. After an unsuccessful attempt to live by writing he began a serious study of modern languages as preparation for the Diplomatic Service. Posted to Constantinople in 1910, he almost immediately contracted tuberculosis, which within five years was to kill him. His achievement as a poet and dramatist within a short career was considerable; he espoused wholeheartedly the doctrine of '*l'art pour l'art*', and avowed himself a disciple of the French Parnassians.

Don Juan in Hell   XV

The night Don Juan came to pay his fees
To Charon, by the caverned water's shore,
A Beggar, proud-eyed as Antisthenes,
Stretched out his knotted fingers on the oar.

Mournful, with drooping breasts and robes unsewn
The shapes of women swayed in ebon skies,
Trailing behind him with a restless moan
Like cattle herded for a sacrifice.

Here, grinning for his wage, stood Sganarelle,
10 And here Don Luis pointed, bent and dim,
To show the dead who lined the holes of Hell,
This was that impious son who mocked at him.

The hollow-eyed, the chaste Elvira came,
Trembling and veiled, to view her traitor spouse.
Was it one last bright smile she thought to claim,
Such as made sweet the morning of his vows?

A great stone man rose like a tower on board,
Stood at the helm and cleft the flood profound:
But the calm hero, leaning on his sword,
20 Gazed back, and would not offer one look round.

(1911)

LORD ALFRED DOUGLAS
(1870–1945)

The third son of the eighth Marquess of Queensberry was educated at
Magdalen College, Oxford. In 1891 he met Oscar Wilde, and it is for
their association from then until Wilde's death in 1900 that Douglas is
now chiefly remembered. Most of his poetry was written during this
and the following decade: for the remainder of his life his energies were
largely consumed in litigation and autobiographical writing concerning
his relationship with Wilde. He was the translator into English of
Wilde's *Salome*. At one time his reputation as a sonneteer was high,
although his longer poems never achieved the same recognition.

La Beauté   XVII

Fair am I, mortals, as a stone-carved dream,
And all men wound themselves against my breast,
The poet's last desire, the loveliest.
Voiceless, eternal as the world I seem.
In the blue air, strange sphinx, I brood supreme
With heart of snow whiter than swan's white crest,
No movement mars the plastic line – I rest
With lips untaught to laugh or eyes to stream.

Singers who see, in trancèd interludes,
10   My splendour set with all superb design,
Consume their days, in toilful ecstasy.
To these revealed, the starry amplitudes
Of my great eyes which make all things divine
Are crystal mirrors of eternity.

(1909)

ARTHUR SYMONS (1865–1945)

The son of a Wesleyan minister, Symons became a leading figure in
London aesthetic circles, befriending W. B. Yeats and the novelist
George Moore, attending meetings of the Rhymers' Club, and collabor-
ating with Aubrey Beardsley on the *Savoy* magazine. A wholehearted
Francophile, he knew Verlaine and Mallarmé and wrote a sympathetic
and pioneering study of symbolism (*The Symbolist Movement in Literature*,
1899). A mental breakdown in 1908 was followed by two years of
confinement and a gradual recovery. He published translations of a few
of the *Petits Poèmes en prose* as early as 1905, but his complete version
of these and of *Les Fleurs du Mal* did not appear until 1925.

This version appears to owe more to Symons's private obsessions than to Baudelaire's text. Phrases like 'not maternal', 'frigid and furtive', 'my gloom', 'my moods of alienation' do not correspond to anything in the original, while Satan, who haunts these lines, does not appear there at all.

La Beauté   XVII

I am beautiful as a dream of stone, but not maternal;
And my breast, where men are slain, none for his learning,
Is made to inspire in the Poet passions that burning
Are mute and carnal as matter and as eternal.

I throne in the azure with Satan, a Sphinx, sound sleeping;
This frigid and furtive heart of mine no man divines;
I hate the movement that displaces the rigid lines:
Satan has never seen me laughing nor even weeping.

The Poets, before the strange attitudes of my gloom,
10   That I assume in my moods of alienation,
In austere studies all their days and nights consume:

Always, when I draw my lovers with my fascination,
There are pure mirrors, wonderful as the nights:
Mine eyes, mine eyes immense – Satan's delights!

(1925)

W. J. ROBERTSON (fl. 1895)

Robertson is known only from his *A Century of French Verse* (1895) which contains biographies and 'experimental translations' of some thirty nineteenth-century poets. Though the collection is uneven, the best of his versions are clear and unforced, and he takes pains to avoid the lazy or unthinking tamperings with the sense of the original that deface so many early translations of Baudelaire; a reviewer in *The Bookman* of July 1895 found his work often laboured, but commendable for its honesty.

Ideal Love   XVIII

No, never can these frail ephemeral creatures,
    The withered offspring of a worthless age,
These buskined limbs, these false and painted features,
    The hunger of a heart like mine assuage.

Leave to the laureate of sickly posies
    Gavarni's hospital sylphs, a simpering choir!
Vainly I seek among those pallid roses
    One blossom that allures my red desire.

Thou with my soul's abysmal dreams be blended,
10   Lady Macbeth, in crime superb and splendid,
    A dream of Æschylus flowered in cold eclipse

Of Northern suns! Thou, Night, inspire my passion,
Calm child of Angelo, coiling in strange fashion
    Thy large limbs moulded for a Titan's lips!

(1895)

GEORGE DILLON

The Giantess   XIX

In times of old when Nature in her glad excess
Brought forth such living marvels as no more are seen,
I should have loved to dwell with a young giantess,
Like a voluptuous cat about the feet of a queen;

To run and laugh beside her in her terrible games,
And see her grow each day to a more fearful size,
And see the flowering of her soul, and the first flames
Of passionate longing in the misty depths of her eyes;

To scale the slopes of her huge knees, explore at will
10   The hollows and the heights of her – and when, oppressed
By the long afternoons of summer, cloudless and still,

She would stretch out across the countryside to rest,
I should have loved to sleep in the shadow of her breast,
Quietly as a village nestling under a hill.

(1936)

W. J. ROBERTSON

The deliberately decadent imagery of this poem is mostly present in the original (though not the 'sandal' of the fifth stanza). It is made more portentous, however, by the choice of *thou* to translate the French *tu*.

Hymn to Beauty   XXI

Be thou from Hell upsprung or Heaven descended,
    Beauty! thy look demoniac and divine
Pours good and evil things confusedly blended,
    And therefore art thou likened unto wine.

Thine eye with dawn is filled, with twilight dwindles,
    Like winds of night thou sprinklest perfumes mild;
Thy kiss, that is a spell, the child's heart kindles,
    Thy mouth, a chalice, makes the man a child.

Fallen from the stars or risen from gulfs of error,
    Fate dogs thy glamoured garments like a slave;
With wanton hands thou scatterest joy and terror,
    And rulest over all, cold as the grave.

Thou tramplest on the dead, scornful and cruel,
    Horror coils like an amulet round thine arms,
Crime on thy superb bosom is a jewel
    That dances amorously among its charms.

The dazzled moth that flies to thee, the candle,
    Shrivels and burns, blessing thy fatal flame;
The lover that dies fawning o'er thy sandal
    Fondles his tomb and breathes the adorëd name.

What if from Heaven or Hell thou com'st, immortal
   Beauty? O sphinx-like monster, since alone
Thine eye, thy smile, thy hand opens the portal
   Of the Infinite I love and have not known.

What if from God or Satan be the evangel?
   Thou my sole Queen! Witch of the velvet eyes!
Since with thy fragrance, rhythm and light, O Angel!
   In a less hideous world time swiftlier flies.

                                (1895)

ARTHUR REED ROPES (1859–1933)

Ropes was a Fellow of King's College, Cambridge. Using the pseudo-nym 'Adrian Ross', he wrote or was involved in upwards of sixty musicals, and adapted a number of Viennese and German operettas (including *The Merry Widow* and *Lilac Time*) for the English stage. He also edited many French classics, and was a founder member of the Performing Right Society. This translation is taken from his *Poems* of 1884.

Strange Perfume   XXII

When, with shut eyes, on some warm autumn night,
   I breathe the perfume of your bosom's heat,
   Before me stretch the lands I long to greet,
Dazzled with beating of monotonous light;
Some sleepy isle where Nature gives to sight
   Strange trees and fruits of savour sharp and sweet,
   Men whose brown limbs are lean and strong and fleet;
Women whose eyes are strangely free and bright.

Drawn by your perfume under magic skies,
10   I see a bay, filled by a fleet that lies
    At rest from waves that wearied it so long;
While the strong scent of the green tamarinds,
Born through my nostrils on the tropic winds,
    Strikes to my soul, mixed with the mariners' song.

                                                    (1884)

ALISTAIR ELLIOT (1932–)

Formerly an actor and a librarian, now a freelance writer, Elliot has published seven collections of English verse, and has translated Euripides, Aristophanes, Verlaine (*Femmes* and *Hombres*) and Heine as well as Baudelaire.

Exotic Scent   XXII

On a warm autumn evening, if I shut both eyes
And breathe the smell of heat from your warm breast,
I see unfolding a long happy coast
That endless sun has burnt into a daze;

An island state of sloth, where nature grows
The strangest trees, and fruits of delicate taste;
Where men are lean and strong, and women rest
Their eyes on one with startling openness.

Following your smell toward this charming zone,
10   I see a harbour full of masts and sails
Still shaken from the ocean waves and winds.

And then the scent of verdant tamarinds
Comes wafting to my heart and swells my nostrils,
Mixed with the shanties of the deep-sea men.

(1991)

J. C. SQUIRE (1884–1958)

Literary knight, honorary ARIBA, cricket-lover, Squire in middle and
old age was thought of as the quintessential English man of letters and
enemy of the avant-garde. His translations of Baudelaire, however,
come from his first published work (*Poems and Baudelaire Flowers*, 1909)
and show him willing to learn from foreign models and already a
versifier of skill and taste.

La Chevelure   XXIII

O billows flowing o'er the shoulders bare!
    O curls! O perfume sweet beyond belief!
Here in this bower to people the night air
With all the memories sleeping in this hair
    I long to shake it like a handkerchief!

Fierce Afric and the languorous Orient,
    All a vast world, distant, nay, almost dead,
Within this aromatic wood is pent;
My soul beloved floats upon thy scent
10   As other souls have music for a bed.

I will go out where full-veined man and tree
   Swoon daylong in the sultry summer's heat –
Strong tresses be the barque which carries me:
Thou holdest a bright dream, O ebon sea,
   Of sails, flames, rowers, on a splendid fleet;

A harbour where through every sense are rolled
   Vast sweeping waves of perfume, sound, and hue,
Where vessels gliding over moire and gold
Stretch up great arms to heaven to enfold
20   The glory of the everlasting blue.

There waits for me delicious drunkenness
   In this dark sea which holds those other seas;
My spirit in the gentle main's caress
Shall know once more the old rich idleness,
   Infinite rockings of embalmèd ease.

Ah! dark-blue, streaming banner of the night,
   You bring me back those azure skies afar,
Plunged in your silken folds my soul takes flight
And drinks once more with measureless delight
30   The scent of cocoa-oil and musk and tar.

For ever I will scatter in each strand,
   That thou may'st never turn deaf ears to me,
Rubies, pearls, sapphires with a lavish hand . . .
Thou art the well-spring in a desert land
   Wherefrom I quaff deep draughts of memory.

(1909)

JEREMY REED (1951–)

Reed has published translations of Montale and von Hardenberg as well as including free versions of Catullus and Horace among his English poems.

This and the next poem greatly exaggerate the indecency of Baudelaire's originals, introducing plain terms or vulgarisms in the place of hints like '*ce jeu singulier*' or '*ce mal où tu te crois savante*'. However, Baudelaire's poems were certainly considered shocking in their day, and Reed perhaps feels he has to try harder to achieve equal shock value with more blasé readers. Lines 16–19 seem to betray a surprising ignorance of the mechanics of conception.

You'd Sleep with Anything   XXV
(after Charles Baudelaire)

You skirt-hitched slut, you'd sleep with anyone
and anything. Boredom makes you perverse
and crave for kicks; you're up all night on drugs.
Your fetish is to bite a heart a day
and leave it bleeding in a used ashtray.
Your eyes light up like a jeweller's display,
or burn like fireworks at a festival,
but lack the moderation to assume
beauty must understate itself or lose.

10   You're nothing but a sex-machine. Your tricks
are vampirical on assorted pricks,
your shamelessness leaves you insensible
to how the mirror frames you as a tart.

But even you in your most private hours
must shrink from what's enacted on your bed,
the long, consummate nights of giving head
to clients, and the one mistake
that catches you My Leather Queen gives birth
incongruously to a child genius

20   who lives to duplicate your ways on earth.

(1992)

JEREMY REED

The Insatiable   XXVI
(after Charles Baudelaire)

Outrageous he-she, skin a cobalt dusk,
an obi's dream, a Faustian mirage,
perfume tinted with Havana and musk,
ebony body made for midnight's stage;

my need for you supersedes opium, wine,
a Nuits-Saint-Georges is nothing to your lips,
my sensual caravan moves like a vine
to ensnare the slow rhythm of your hips.

Your dark eyes are skylights into your mind,
10   my body's branded by your raging flame,
a Styxian sailor set out to find

the nine circular loops across the flood,
and burn in the underworld where you tame
tigers attracted to your boiling blood.

(1990)

RICHARD HOWARD

Sed Non Satiata   XXVI

Daughter of darkness, slattern deity
rank with musk and nicotine, the spawn
of filthy covens or a shaman's rites
ebony fetish, nameless talisman . . . And yet

to wine, to opium even, I prefer
the elixir of your lips on which love flaunts
itself; and in the wasteland of desire
your eyes afford the wells to slake my thirst.

Seal them, those sooty holes from which your soul
10   rains hellfire too, relentless sorceress!
I am no Styx, to cradle you nine times.

alas! and cannot with some Fury's lust,
to break your spirit and your heart, become
in your bed's inferno . . . Persephone!

(1982)

PETER DALE (1938–)

A noted translator of French poetry, Dale was co-editor of *Agenda* for many years. His versions of Villon and Laforgue attracted much praise for their resourceful and probing fidelity.

Undulant and Opalescent the Robes   XXVII

Undulant and opalescent the robes on her
So even when she walks you'd think of dance,
Like those long serpents holy charmers stir
In rhythm as their swaying wands entrance.

Like desert azure and the barren sand,
With no sense of the suffering human throng,
Like rising seas whose lengthy webs expand,
With such indifference she sweeps along.

Her polished eyes are made of precious stone
And in that nature now, symbolic, strange,
Where sphinx and taintless angel interchange,

Where all is gold, steel, light and gems alone,
Glints like a useless star eternally,
The sterile woman's chilling majesty.

(1985)

RICHARD HERNE SHEPHERD
(1842–95)

A bibliographer and editor, Shepherd produced numerous trade editions of English writers and gained a certain notoriety by issuing pirated collections of early works by Tennyson and Elizabeth Barrett Browning, the first of which was suppressed by injunction. His *Translations from Charles Baudelaire, with a few original poems* (1869) contains just three translations of Baudelaire, marooned among Shepherd's own verses. Their chief distinction is that of being the earliest known translations of Baudelaire's poetry into English. His translation of 'Une Charogne' is awkward in places, but pulls itself together to deliver a very neat and accurate handling of the last three stanzas, whose rhetoric has defeated more than one more-celebrated translator.

A Carcass   XXIX

Recall to mind the sight we saw, my soul,
    That soft, sweet summer day:
Upon a bed of flints a carrion foul,
    Just as we turn'd the way,

Its legs erected, wanton-like, in air,
    Burning and sweating pest,
In unconcern'd and cynic sort laid bare
    To view its noisome breast.

The sun lit up the rottenness with gold,
10   To bake it well inclined,
And give great Nature back a hundredfold
    All she together join'd.

The sky regarded as the carcass proud
   Oped flower-like to the day;
So strong the odour, on the grass you vow'd
   You thought to faint away.

The flies the putrid belly buzz'd about,
   Whence black battalions throng
Of maggots, like thick liquid flowing out
20   The living rags along.

And as a wave they mounted and went down,
   Or darted sparkling wide;
As if the body, by a wild breath blown,
   Lived as it multiplied.

From all this life a music strange there ran,
   Like wind and running burns;
Or like the wheat a winnower in his fan
   With rhythmic movement turns.

The forms wore off, and as a dream grew faint,
30   An outline dimly shown,
And which the artist finishes to paint
   From memory alone.

Behind the rocks watch'd us with angry eye
   A bitch disturb'd in theft,
Waiting to take, till we had pass'd her by,
   The morsel she had left.

Yet you will be like that corruption too,
   Like that infection prove –
Star of my eyes, sun of my nature, you,
40   My angel and my love!

Queen of the graces, you will even be so,
    When, the last ritual said,
Beneath the grass and the fat flowers you go,
    To mould among the dead.

Then, O my beauty, tell the insatiate worm,
    Who wastes you with his kiss,
I have kept the godlike essence and the form
    Of perishable bliss!

(1869)

H. C.

H. C., who published a collection of Baudelaire translations in 1894 is usually identified with Henry Curwen, who had published a much shorter selection in his *Echoes from the French Poets* (1870). Their styles are fairly dissimilar, however; H. C.'s rhythms are not so ponderous.

The Vampire   XXXI

O thou, who, as a sharp-edged brand,
Hast in my heart an entrance made,
Thou, who, resistless as a band
Of demons with wild charms arrayed,

Hast of my spirit, lost to pride,
Fashioned thy bed and thy domain.
Polluted wretch! to whom I'm tied,
As is the convict to his chain.

As reckless gambler to his play,
10   Or as the drunkard to his wine,
Or vermin to their putrid prey,
Thee! to all curses I consign.

Quick dealing swords I often prayed
To conquer me my liberty,
To treacherous poison oft I said, –
Strength to my coward heart supply.

Alas! the poison and the sword
With scornful speech my prayer withstood,
You are too base to be restored
20   From your accursed servitude.

Weak fool! if pitying your state,
We freed you from her shameful chain,
Your kisses would resuscitate
The vampire's body once again.

(1894)

F. P. STURM

The Balcony   XXXVI

Mother of memories, mistress of mistresses,
O thou, my pleasure, thou, all my desire,
Thou shalt recall the beauty of caresses,
The charm of evenings by the gentle fire,
Mother of memories, mistress of mistresses!

The eves illumined by the burning coal,
The balcony where veiled rose-vapour clings –
How soft your breast was then, how sweet your soul!
Ah, and we said imperishable things,
10   Those eves illumined by the burning coal.

Lovely the suns were in those twilights warm,
And space profound, and strong life's pulsing flood;
In bending o'er you, queen of every charm,
I thought I breathed the perfume of your blood.
The suns were beauteous in those twilights warm.

The film of night flowed round and over us,
And my eyes in the dark did your eyes meet;
I drank your breath, ah! sweet and poisonous,
And in my hands fraternal slept your feet –
20   Night, like a film, flowed round and over us.

I can recall those happy days forgot,
And see, with head bowed on your knees, my past.
Your languid beauties now would move me not
Did not your gentle heart and body cast
The old spell of those happy days forgot.

Can vows and perfume, kisses infinite,
Be reborn from the gulf we cannot sound;
As rise to heaven suns once again made bright
After being plunged in deep seas and profound?
30   Ah, vows and perfumes, kisses infinite!

(1906)

ROY CAMPBELL

The Possessed   XXXVII

The sun in crêpe has muffled up his fire.
Moon of my life! Half shade yourself like him.
Slumber or smoke. Be silent and be dim,
And in the gulf of boredom plunge entire;

I love you thus! However, if you like,
Like some bright star from its eclipse emerging,
To flaunt with Folly where the crowds are surging –
Flash, lovely dagger, from your sheath and strike!

Light up your eyes from chandeliers of glass!
10 Light up the lustful looks of louts that pass!
Morbid or petulant, I thrill before you.

Be what you will, black night or crimson dawn;
No fibre of my body tautly drawn,
But cries: 'Beloved demon, I adore you!'

(1952)

LEWIS PIAGET SHANKS
(1878–1935)

Shanks was Professor of French at Johns Hopkins University from 1925 to 1935. He wrote books on Flaubert and Anatole France and a very good literary biography of Baudelaire, *Baudelaire: Flesh and Spirit* (1930). His *Flowers of Evil* (1926), the first American translation of a sizeable number of Baudelaire's poems, is in album format, with very wide margins, few capital letters, a mauve and silver art deco cover and weak if mildly improper illustrations in a sub-cubist style. Amid so much modernity Shanks's diction sometimes recalls the previous century ('artists blind', 'grows apace' and so forth), but his renderings are accurate, his management of metre and rhyme usually deft, and from time to time he coins a truly memorable line.

Un Fantôme   XXXVIII

i
LES TÉNÈBRES

down in the unplumbed crypt of blight
where Fate abandoned me to die,
where falls no cheering ray; where I,
sole lodger of the sulky Night,

like artists blind God sets apart
in mockery – I paint the murk;
where, like a ghoulish cook at work,
I boil and munch upon my heart,

momently gleams, and grows apace,
10   a phantom languorously bright,
and by its dreamy Orient grace,

when it attains its radiant height,
at last I know the lovely thing:
'tis She! girl black yet glimmering.

ii
LE PARFUM

how long, in silken favours, last
their prisoned scents! how greedily
we breathe the incense-grain, a sea
of fragrance, in cathedrals vast!

o deep enchanting sorcery!
20   in present joys to find the past!
'tis thus on cherished flesh amassed
Love culls the flower of memory.

her thick curled hair, like bags of musk
or living censers, left the dusk
with strange wild odours all astir,

and, from her lace and velvet busk,
– candid and girlish, over her,
hovered a heavy scent of fur.

iii
LE CADRE

as framing to a portrait gives
30   – though from a famous brush it be –
a magic full of mystery
secluding it from all that lives,

so gems, divans, gold, steel became
her beauty's border and attire;
no pomp obscured its perfect fire,
all seemed to serve her as a frame.

one even might have said she found
all sought to love her, for she drowned
in kisses of her silks and laces,

40   her fair nude body, all a-quiver,
and swift or slow, each pose would give her
a host of girlish simian graces.

iv
LE PORTRAIT

Death and Disease to ashes turn
all flames that wrapped our youth around.
of her soft eyes, so quick to burn,
her mouth, wherein my heart was drowned,

of her wild kisses' tyrannies,
her passion's blaze implacable –
drear heart! what now is left of these?
50   only a faded old pastel

dying, like me, in loneliness,
duller each day in every part,
stripped by Time's pinion merciless . . .

black murderer of life and art,
never shalt thou destroy in me
her, once my pride and ecstasy!

(1926)

VERNON WATKINS (1906–67)

Watkins, a Welshman, was educated at Magdalene College, Cambridge and then spent most of his working life as a bank clerk in Swansea. He was a close friend of Dylan Thomas, whose letters to him were published shortly after Thomas's death. Although Thomas was an influence on and a source of encouragement to Watkins, Yeats and the European Symbolists and Romantics were at least as important to him. He produced notable translations of Heine and Hölderlin, poets with whom he expressed an affinity in his own verse. His versions of Baudelaire are fewer and less empathetic: Baudelaire's savage negations are a long way from Watkins's natural territory. None the less he responds to the assertiveness of 'Je te donne ces vers . . .' with finely judged rhetoric: with his characteristic metrical ambiguities, his lines shifting from tetrameter to hexameter, and supported by rich alliteration, he offers a convincing solution to the imitation in English of the alexandrine's expansiveness and poise.

I Offer You This Verse . . .   XXXIX

I offer you this verse so that if once my name
Beaches with good fortune on epochs far away
And makes the minds of men dream at the close of day,
Vessel to whose assistance a great tempest came,

The memory of you, like fables indistinct,
May weary the reader like a tympanum's refrain,
And by a fraternal and most mystical chain
Still seem as though hanging, to my lofty rhymes linked;

Accurst being to whom, from the depth of the abyss
10   To the height of the sky, nothing but me responds!
– O you who like a shade whose trace none may retard

Trample with a light foot and a serene regard
The mortal dolts who judged you bringer of bitterness,
Statue with eyes of jet, great angel browed with bronze!

(1977)

RICHARD HOWARD

Suppose My Name . . .   XXXIX

Suppose my name were favored by the winds,
my voyage prospered, and the future read
all that I wrote, and marveled . . . Love, they're yours!
I give you poems to make your memory

echo the way archaic legends do,
so that by some incantatory spell,
haunting the reader like a psaltery,
you will be caught within my cadences;

who now, from Pit to Empyrean scorned
10   by all but me, have simply walked away
and left no trace but shadows as you pass,

staring in mute composure at a world
that stupidly reviles your unconcern,
my jet-eyed statue, angel with brazen brows!

(1982)

GEORGE DILLON

All, All   XLI

The Devil up my attic stair
Came tiptoeing a while ago
And, trying to catch me unaware,
Said laughing, 'I should like to know,

'Of all her many charms, what springs
Most often to your mind? Of all
The rose-coloured and shadowy things
Whereby her beauty may enthrall,

'Which is the sweetest?' – O my soul,
You answered the abhorrèd Guest:
Her beauty is complete and whole.
No single part is loveliest.

'When she is near, I cannot say
What gives me such intense delight.
She dazzles like the break of day,
She comforts like the fall of night.

'My senses seem to merge in one;
The harmony that rules her being
Is all my knowledge – I have none
Of hearing, smelling, touching, seeing.

'No, no. I cannot make a choice
In this sublime bewilderment.
Perhaps the music of her scent!
Perhaps the perfume of her voice!'

(1936)

F. P. STURM

The title, 'Réversibilité', refers to the doctrine according to which the merits of one human being can, if God so wills, be 'diverted' and help to save another.

Reversibility   XLIV

Angel of gaiety, have you tasted grief?
Shame and remorse and sobs and weary spite,
And the vague terrors of the fearful night
That crush the heart up like a crumpled leaf?
Angel of gaiety, have you tasted grief?

Angel of kindness, have you tasted hate?
With hands clenched in the dark, and tears of gall,
When Vengeance beats her hellish battle-call,
And makes herself the captain of our fate,
10   Angel of kindness, have you tasted hate?

Angel of health, did ever you know pain,
Which like an exile trails his tired footfalls
The cold length of the whole infirmary walls,
With lips compressed, seeking the sun in vain?
Angel of health, did ever you know pain?

Angel of beauty, do you wrinkles know?
Know you the fear of age, the torment vile
Of reading secret horror in the smile
Of eyes your eyes have loved since long ago?
20   Angel of beauty, do you wrinkles know?

Angel of happiness, and joy, and light,
Old David would have asked for youth afresh
From the pure touch of your enchanted flesh;
I but implore your prayers to aid my plight,
Angel of happiness, and joy, and light.

(1906)

JOHN GOUDGE (1921–   )

Goudge was born in India and his war service was there and in Burma,
with the Gurkhas. A selection from his complete translation of *Les
Fleurs du Mal* was published in 1979; he has also translated Aragon and
Nerval.

The informal anapaestic metre used here and in XC below gives an
odd, colloquial sound to his renderings which recalls Irish parlour ballads
('Believe me, if all those endearing young charms . . .') and seems
somehow appropriate to this story, most untypical in Baudelaire, of a
shared moment of intimacy and trust.

Confession   XLV

Just once and once only, sweet lady and kind,
        You leant your smooth arm on my arm
(And down in the darkest depth of my mind
        The memory of this is still warm):

It was late; like a medal, new-minted and bright,
    The moon in her fulness was gleaming,
And solemn and deep as a river the night
    Over sleeping Paris was streaming.

And cats by the houses through carriage gates crept
10   And passed us furtively by
With ears pricked, or like ghosts of departed friends kept
    Us measured company.

In the colourless light, free and intimate,
    We were talking, when suddenly,
Your rich sonorous chords that used to vibrate
    With radiant gaiety

Like a fanfare of joy in the sparkling air
    Of morning, gave out a note –
A note that was plaintive, unusual, queer
20   And quavering fled from your throat.

Like a mean little child, horrid, sulky, unclean,
    Whose family blush to reveal,
And whom, many years by the world unseen,
    In a cellar they've tried to conceal.

And this shrill note of yours, my poor angel, it cries,
    'There is nothing sure on this earth,
And man's greed and self-love, in whatever disguise,
    Will always reveal their true worth.

'As for beautiful women, what an arduous calling!
30   And dancers, how trivial their toil!
Dull, cold, and tired to the point of falling,
    They still smile a mechanical smile.

'And building on hearts is a profitless thing:
    Nothing's solid, not love nor beauty.
Until Death and Oblivion pluck them and fling
    Them back to Eternity.'

And I often remember the enchanted moon's glow,
    The silence, the languor and all,
And that horrible confidence whispered so low
40   In the heart's confessional.

(1979)

J. C. SQUIRE

The Spiritual Dawn   XLVI

When upon revellers the stained dawn breaks
    The fierce ideal comes with it; at that hour,
    Stirred by some terrible avenging power,
An angel in the sated brute awakes.

Above the stricken, suffering man there glow
    Far azure plains of unimagined bliss
    Which draw his dreaming spirit like the abyss.
O pure, beloved Goddess, even so

O'er the smoked wrecks of stupid scenes of shame
10   Brighter and rosier thy sweet memory
    Hovers before my wide eyes hauntingly . . .

The Sun has dimmed and charred the candles' flame,
   And thus, my glorious all-conquering one,
   Thy shade is peer to the immortal Sun.

(1909)

Harmonie du Soir

Of all Baudelaire's poems this is perhaps the one that depends most on sound-patterning. Debussy's setting of it is appropriately lush. It has tempted numerous English translators, perhaps drawn on by the difficulty of capturing the hypnotic patterns of the original in a language with a different system of vowels and stresses.

We print three of the better versions. *Pace* Reeves and Forbes, an *ostensoir* is not a chalice but, as Douglas says, a monstrance – an object made to display the consecrated host to the faithful during a religious ceremony.

Harmonie du Soir   XLVII

Voici venir les temps où vibrant sur sa tige
Chaque fleur s'évapore ainsi qu'un encensoir;
Les sons et les parfums tournent dans l'air du soir;
Valse mélancolique et langoureux vertige!

Chaque fleur s'évapore ainsi qu'un encensoir;
Le violon frémit comme un cœur qu'on afflige;
Valse mélancolique et langoureux vertige!
Le ciel est triste et beau comme un grand reposoir.

Le violon frémit comme un cœur qu'on afflige,
10   *Un cœur tendre, qui hait le néant vaste et noir!*
Le ciel est triste et beau comme un grand reposoir;
Le soleil s'est noyé dans son sang qui se fige.

Un cœur tendre, qui hait le néant vaste et noir,
Du passé lumineux recueille tout vestige!
Le soleil s'est noyé dans son sang qui se fige . . .
Ton souvenir en moi luit comme un ostensoir!

LORD ALFRED DOUGLAS

Harmonie du Soir   XLVII

Now is the hour when, swinging in the breeze,
Each flower, like a censer, sheds its sweet.
The air is full of scents and melodies,
O languorous waltz! O swoon of dancing feet!

Each flower, like a censer, sheds its sweet,
The violins are like sad souls that cry,
O languorous waltz! O swoon of dancing feet!
A shrine of Death and Beauty is the sky.

The violins are like sad souls that cry,
10   Poor souls that hate the vast black night of Death;
A shrine of Death and Beauty is the sky.
Drowned in red blood, the Sun gives up his breath.

This soul that hates the vast black night of Death
Takes all the luminous past back tenderly.
Drowned in red blood, the Sun gives up his breath.
Thine image like a monstrance shines in me.

(1899)

JAMES REEVES (1909–1978)

Reeves was a teacher and an energetic editor of poetry. Martin Seymour-Smith wrote that 'Guilt, regret, anger, desire for stability . . . are among the staple elements in Reeves's best poetry' – as they are in Baudelaire's.

Harmonies of Evening   XLVII

These are the moments when on vibrant stems
The flowers yield up their being like a censer.
Perfumes and sounds eddy upon the air
– A melancholy dance, a whirling languor.

The flowers yield up their being like a censer.
The violin shudders like a heart in torment
– A melancholy dance, a whirling languor.
The sky's sad beauty is a pilgrim's rest.

The violin shudders like a heart in torment,
10   A tender heart hating the black abyss.
The sky's sad beauty is a pilgrim's rest.
In its own stiffening blood the sun is drowned.

A tender heart hating the black abyss
Gathers all remnants of the luminous past.
In its own stiffening blood the sun is drowned.
Your memory glows within me like a chalice.

(1972)

DUNCAN FORBES (1947–   )

Forbes was formerly Head of English at Cheltenham College. His
poems have won a Gregory Award and he has so far published three
collections. His translation of 'Harmonie du Soir' is published here for
the first time.

Harmonie du Soir   XLVII

Here comes the time when vibrant on its stem
Each flower is misty like a censer flame;
The sounds and perfumes turn in evening air;
A melancholy waltz and languid blur.

Each flower is misty like a censer flame;
The cello trembles like a heart in pain;
A melancholy waltz and languid blur!
The sky is sad and lovely like a shrine.

The cello trembles like a heart in pain,
10   A tender heart, which hates the vast black void!
The sky is sad and lovely like a shrine;
The sun is drowning in congealing blood.

A tender heart which hates the vast black void
Collects each vestige of a past which gleams.
The sun is drowning in congealing blood . . .
In me your memory like a chalice shines.

(1997)

LEWIS PIAGET SHANKS

Le Flacon   XLVIII

so keen some fragrances, they freely pass
all barriers.   they would pierce a wall of glass.
unlatch a coffer from the Orient
whose creaking hinge will scarcely grant consent,

or cupboard in an empty house, where murk,
sharp smells and cobwebs of a century lurk,
thou'lt find perhaps a flask that holds a host
of memories, free perchance a living ghost.

crushed in the gloom a thousand keepsakes lay
10   like coffined larvae there, which, quivering, grey,
released at last arise on soaring wing,
rose-flushed or azure, golden, glittering,

and swirling memories mount, to thrill and tease
our closing eyes; we reel in murk, as these
grapple amain and hurl the quailing soul
down to a Pit where human odours roll

and fell it on the brink that waits for all,
where, bursting, Lazarus-like, its rotted pall,
stirs and awakes the spectral visage of
20   a charming, fusty, weird, forgotten love.

so when Oblivion blots my memory dim,
and in a corner of a cupboard grim
I lie cast off, a sorry flask and old,
crackled and dusty, viscous, green with mould,

I'll be thy coffin, lovely pestilence!
I'll prove thy power and thy virulence,
dear poison brewed by angels! dulcet fire
I've drunk, my life, my death, my heart's desire!

(1926)

ALAN CONDER (1884–1953)

An Englishman, born and educated in Leeds, he was a violinist and
quartet leader as well as a translator. He published a complete version
of *Les Fleurs du Mal* the year before his death.

The Cat   LI

i

A cat is walking in my brain
As in his room – a gentle, strong
And charming cat whose miauling song
Is so discreet as to remain

Well-nigh inaudible; but calm
Or querulous, no matter which,
His voice is always deep and rich.
There is his secret and his charm.

In strains that ripple and that filter
10   Throughout my darkest being, he
Enchants me as with poetry,
Or with the magic of some philtre.

His voice can lull the cruellest ill;
All ecstasies are in its range;
Long though the phrases be, his strange
Song without words can work its spell.

No, there is no bow that can sing
Upon that instrument, my heart,
And make such royal music start
20   From its most thrilling, vibrant string

As thou, cat, with thy witchery,
Seraphic creature, mystical,
In whom, as in an angel, all
Is harmony and subtlety.

ii

The magic perfume of the cat
Is such that, having stroked the fur
Of mine but once, I was aware
That I too was perfumed by it.

The genius of the place is he,
30   Inspirer, judge of his domain,
Where no one may dispute his reign.
Is he some sprite or deity?

When from my dear cat's eyes that chain
Me like a magnet mine return,
And with docility in turn
They peer into my soul again,

To my astonishment I see
Pale pupils pouring out their rays;
Bright beacons, living opals, gaze
40   And contemplate me fixedly.

(1952)

ARTHUR SYMONS

Symons's versions are usually so unreliable that here and elsewhere
we accompany them with a plain prose translation of the original by
CC.

'Vair' in the fifth stanza is a kind of fur – rare attire indeed for
dancing-girls!

The Beautiful Ship   LII

My desire is to respire thy charms that are divine
And all in thee that is more beautiful than wine,
All this desire of mine
Is to paint the child whose fashions are malign.*

* I want to tell you, o soft enchantress, of the varied beauties which adorn
your young body; I wish to paint for you your beauty, where childhood
joins with maturity.

When thou dost wander thy skirt balances to and fro
In the wind's embraces from the seas that flow,
I see in thee a painted show
Following an ardent rhythm, languid and slow.★

On thy large neck, so pure and undefiled,
Thy dear head flaunts itself like dancers, wild,
And I the Exiled
Follow thy subtle footsteps, majestic child!†

My desire is to respire thy charms that are divine
And all in thee that is more beautiful than wine,
All this desire of mine
Is to paint the child whose fashions are malign.

Thine ardent breasts advance to meet the air
Triumphant as the silk that hides them and rare
As dancing-girls in vair
That leave thee to the winds that are most fair.‡

Provoking breasts, with their red points of roses!
Secret to none, as any shy rose that uncloses,
Where perfume with scent dozes
Delirious to the hearts wherein no rest reposes!¶

★ When you go along, sweeping the air with your wide skirt, you have
the look of a fine vessel putting out to sea, laden with sail, and rolling in
a gentle rhythm, lazy and slow.
† On your broad, round neck, on your plump shoulders, your head bears
itself high, with strange, graceful airs; placid and triumphant, you go your
way, majestic child.
‡ Your thrusting bosom, pushing at the silk, your triumphant bosom is a
fine cupboard whose panels, convex and bright, are like shields catching
shafts of light.
¶ Provoking shields, armed with pink points! Cupboard with sweet secrets,
full of good things, of wines, of perfumes, of cordials which would drive
brains and hearts wild!

When thou dost wander thy skirt balances to and fro
In the wind's embraces from the seas that flow,
I see in thee a painted show
Following an ardent rhythm, languid and slow.

Thy noble legs under their draperies bewitching
30   Torment obscure desires, set my nerves twitching,
Like two Sorcerers pitching
Black drugs to a snake whose ardent coils are itching.★

Thy lovely arms that wave luxuriously
Like unto shining coiling boas furiously
Press one's heart obstinately
And leave me, thy Lover, lonely as the Sea.†

On thy large neck, so pure and undefiled,
Thy dear head flaunts itself like dancers, wild,
And I the Exiled
40   Follow thy subtle footsteps, majestic child!

(1925)

★ Your noble legs, under the flounces which they drive along, torment
hidden desires and stir them up, like two witches turning a black philtre
in a deep vessel.
† Your arms, which would make short work of a precocious Hercules,
are solid rivals to gleaming boa constrictors, made to squeeze your lover
unyieldingly, as if to leave his impression on your heart.

L'Invitation au Voyage

Like 'Harmonie du Soir', this is one of Baudelaire's most famously musical poems. Settings exist by Chabrier and Duparc. There is a prose version of the same theme in the *Petits Poèmes en prose.*

L'Invitation au Voyage LIII

Mon enfant, ma sœur,
Songe à la douceur
D'aller là-bas vivre ensemble!
Aimer à loisir,
Aimer et mourir
Au pays qui te ressemble!
Les soleils mouillés
De ces ciels brouillés
Pour mon esprit ont les charmes
Si mystérieux
De tes traîtres yeux,
Brillant à travers leurs larmes.

Là, tout n'est qu'ordre et beauté,
Luxe, calme et volupté.

Des meubles luisants,
Polis par les ans,
Décoreraient notre chambre;
Les plus rares fleurs
Mêlant leurs odeurs
Aux vagues senteurs de l'ambre,
Les riches plafonds,
Les miroirs profonds,
La splendeur orientale,

    Tout y parlerait
      A l'âme en secret
  Sa douce langue natale.

  Là, tout n'est qu'ordre et beauté,
  Luxe, calme et volupté.

      Vois sur ces canaux
30   Dormir ces vaisseaux
  Dont l'humeur est vagabonde;
      C'est pour assouvir
      Ton moindre désir
  Qu'ils viennent du bout du monde.
      — Les soleils couchants
      Revêtent les champs,
  Les canaux, la ville entière,
      D'hyacinthe et d'or;
      Le monde s'endort
40 Dans une chaude lumière.

  Là, tout n'est qu'ordre et beauté,
  Luxe, calme et volupté.

J. C. SQUIRE

The Invitation to the Voyage   LIII

    How sweet, my own,
      Could we live alone
  Over beyond the sea!
      To love and to die
      Indolently
  In the land that's akin to thee!

Where the suns which rise
        In the watery skies
Weave soft spells over my sight,
10   As thy false eyes do
        When they flicker through
Their tears with a dim, strange light.

There all is beauty and symmetry,
Pleasure and calm and luxury.

        Years that have gone
        Have polished and shone
The things that would fill our room;
        The flowers most rare
        Which scent the air
20 In the richly-ceiling'd gloom,
        And the mirrors profound,
        And the walls around
With Orient splendour hung,
        To the soul would speak
        Of things she doth seek
In her gentle native tongue.

There is all beauty and symmetry,
Pleasure and calm and luxury.

        The canals are deep
30   Where the strange ships sleep
Far from the land of their birth;
        To quench the fire
        Of thy least desire
They have come from the ends of the earth.

The sunsets drown
Peaceful town
And meadow, and stagnant stream
In bistre and gold,
And the world enfold
40   In a warm and luminous dream.

There all is beauty and symmetry,
Pleasure and calm and luxury.

(1909)

EDNA ST VINCENT MILLAY

Invitation to the Voyage   LIII

Think, would it not be
Sweet to live with me
All alone, my child, my love? –
Sleep together, share
All things, in that fair
Country you remind me of?
Charming in the dawn
There, the half-withdrawn
Drenched, mysterious sun appears
10   In the curdled skies,
Treacherous as your eyes
Shining from behind their tears.

There, restraint and order bless
Luxury and voluptuousness.

We should have a room
Never out of bloom:
Tables polished by the palm
Of the vanished hours
Should reflect rare flowers
20   In that amber-scented calm;
Ceilings richly wrought,
Mirrors deep as thought,
Walks with eastern splendour hung, –
All should speak apart
To the homesick heart
In its own dear native tongue.

There, restraint and order bless
Luxury and voluptuousness.

See, their voyage past,
30   To their moorings fast,
On the still canals asleep.
These big ships; to bring
You some trifling thing
They have braved the furious deep.
– Now the sun goes down,
Tinting dyke and town,
Field, canal, all things in sight,
Hyacinth and gold;
All that we behold
40   Slumbers in its ruddy light.

There, restraint and order bless
Luxury and voluptuousness.

(1936)

RICHARD WILBUR

L'Invitation au Voyage   LIII

> My child, my sister,
>   dream
> How sweet all things would seem
> Were we in that kind land to live together,
>   And there love slow and long,
>   There love and die among
> Those scenes that image you, that sumptuous weather.
>   Drowned suns that glimmer there
>   Through cloud-disheveled air
> Move me with such a mystery as appears
>   Within those other skies
>   Of your treacherous eyes
> When I behold them shining through their tears.
>
> There, there is nothing else but grace and measure,
> Richness, quietness, and pleasure.
>
>   Furniture that wears
>   The lustre of the years
> Softly would glow within our glowing chamber,
>   Flowers of rarest bloom
>   Proffering their perfume
> Mixed with the vague fragrances of amber;
>   Gold ceilings would there be,
>   Mirrors deep as the sea,
> The walls all in an Eastern splendor hung –
>   Nothing but should address
>   The soul's loneliness,
> Speaking her sweet and secret native tongue.

There, there is nothing else but grace and measure,
Richness, quietness, and pleasure.

30   See, sheltered from the swells
          There in the still canals
Those drowsy ships that dream of sailing forth;
          It is to satisfy
          Your least desire, they ply
Hither through all the waters of the earth.
          The sun at close of day
          Clothes the fields of hay,
Then the canals, at last the town entire
          In hyacinth and gold:
40   Slowly the land is rolled
Sleepward under a sea of gentle fire.

There, there is nothing else but grace and measure,
Richness, quietness, and pleasure.

(1955)

RICHARD HOWARD

Autumnal   LVI

i

Soon cold shadows will close over us
and summer's transitory gold be gone;
I hear them chopping firewood in our court –
the dreary thud of logs on cobblestone.

Winter will come to repossess my soul
with rage and outrage, horror, drudgery,
and like the sun in its polar holocaust
my heart will be a block of blood-red ice.

I listen trembling to that grim tattoo –
10   build a gallows, it would sound the same.
My mind becomes a tower giving way
under the impact of a battering-ram.

Stunned by the strokes, I seem to hear, somewhere,
a coffin hurriedly hammered shut – for whom?
Summer was yesterday; autumn is here!
Strange how that sound rings out like a farewell.

ii

How sweet the greenish light of your long eyes!
But even that turns bitter now, and nothing
– not love, the boudoir, nor its busy hearth –
20   can match the summer's radiance on the sea.

Love me still, my darling! mother me,
ungrateful though I am, your naughty boy.
Sister and mistress! be the fleeting warmth
of a sumptuous autumn or a setting sun.

Your chore will be brief – the grave is covetous!
so let me rest my forehead on your knees
and relish, as I mourn white summer's lapse,
the yellow favor of the waning year.

(1982)

JAMES MCGOWAN (1937–   )

James McGowan is Professor of English at Wesleyan University, Bloom-
ington, Illinois. He published *66 Translations from Charles Baudelaire* in
1985, and was then asked to translate the whole of the *Fleurs du Mal*
for the World's Classics series. His version appeared in 1993.

Mœsta et errabunda   LXII

Agatha, tell me, could your heart take flight
From this black city, from this filthy sea
Off to some other sea, where splendour might
Burst blue and clear – a new virginity?
Agatha, tell me, could your heart take flight?

The vast sea offers comfort in our pain!
What demon lets the ocean's raucous cry
Above the great wind-organ's grumbling strain
Perform the holy rite of lullaby?
10   The vast sea offers comfort in our pain!

Frigate or wagon, carry me away!
Away from where the mud is made of tears!
– Agatha, can your sad heart sometimes say:
Far from the crimes, remorse, the grief of years,
Frigate or wagon, carry me away!

How distant are you, perfumed paradise,
Where lovers play beneath the blue above,
Where hearts may drown themselves in pure delights,
Where what one loves is worthy to be loved!
20   How distant are you, perfumed paradise!

But the green paradise of youthful loves,
The games and songs, the kisses, the bouquets,
The violins that sing in hilly groves,
The evening cups of wine in shady ways,
– But the green paradise of youthful loves,

The sinless paradise of stolen joys,
Is it already far beyond the seas?
Can we recall it with our plaintive voice,
And give it life with silver melodies,
30   The sinless paradise of stolen joys?

(1993)

ROY FULLER (1912–91)

Fuller trained as a solicitor and spent his working life with the Woolwich
Equitable Building Society, of which he became a director in 1969; he
was also (1972–9) a governor of the BBC. His long and illustrious
career as novelist and poet – crowned with the Oxford Professorship
of Poetry (1968–73) and the Queen's Gold Medal for Poetry (1970) –
perhaps drew strength from the rationality and mental discipline of a
distinguished business career.

Though he was early associated with the political poets of the 1930s,
and after the war was often linked to (though never formally associated
with) the kitchen-sink realism of the Movement, the cultivated, sceptical
manner of much of his poetry is not so far removed from that urbane
strand in American letters which has produced some of the finest
translations in this anthology, such as those by Anthony Hecht and
Richard Wilbur; there is perhaps a little more steel in Fuller's work, a
darker sense of human limitation and of the burden of history.

Cats   LXVI

Lovers and austere dons are equally
(In their maturity) attached to cats –
Cats soft but cruel, emperors of flats,
Touchy like these and like those sedentary.

Friends of the sensual, the cerebral,
They seek the quiet and horror of the dark;
If they had ever bent their pride to work
They might have pulled the funeral cars of hell.

Asleep they take the noble attitude
10   Of the great sphinxes that appear to brood,
Stretched in the wastes, in dreams that have no end.

Their loins are electric with fecundity,
And particles of gold, like finest sand,
Star vaguely their unfathomable eye.

(1954)

Owls   LXVII

Swaddled in yews as black as ink
The owls sit in a tidy frieze
Like oriental deities,
Unlidding their red eyes. They think.

They will sit on quite motionless
Until that hour, nostalgic, dun,
When, rolling up the slanting sun,
Shadows reoccupy the place.

Their attitude reminds the clever
10   That in our time and world one never
Ought to seek action, or revolt;

Man shaken by a creeping shade
Bears always in himself the guilt
Of having wished to change his fate.

(1954)

ROBERT FITZGERALD (1910–85)

Fitzgerald was educated at Harvard, and after some years as a journalist on *Time* magazine, took up a professorship of creative writing at Princeton and subsequently at Harvard. Several volumes of his poetry have appeared; he also translated the *Odyssey* (1961, Bollingen Prize) and the *Iliad* (1974), as well as plays by Euripides and Sophocles (in collaboration).

Baudelaire's Music   LXIX

On music drawn away, a sea-borne mariner,
    Star over bowsprit pale,
Beneath a roof of mist or depths of lucid air
    I put out under sail;

Breastbone my steady bow and lungs full, running free
    Before a following gale,
I ride the rolling back and mass of every sea
    By Night wrapt in her veil;

All passions and all joys that vessels undergo
10   Tremble alike in me;
Fair winds or waves in havoc when the tempests blow

     On the enormous sea
Rock me, and level calms come silvering sea and air,
     A glass for my despair.

     (1971)

RICHARD HOWARD

The Happy Corpse   LXXII

Wherever the soil is rich and full of snails
I want to dig myself a nice deep grave –
deep enough to stretch out these old bones
and sleep in peace, like a shark in the cradling wave.

Testaments and tombstones always lie!
Before collecting such official grief,
I'd rather ask the crows, while I'm alive,
to pick my carcass clean from end to end.

They may be deaf and blind, my friends the worms,
10   yet surely they will welcome a happy corpse;
feasting philosophers, scions of decay.

eat your way through me without a second thought
and let me know if one last twinge is left
for a soulless body deader than the dead!

     (1982)

J. C. SQUIRE

The Cracked Bell   LXXIV

'Tis bitter-sweet, when winter nights are long,
  To watch, beside the flames which smoke and twist,
The distant memories which slowly throng,
  Brought by the chime soft-singing through the mist.

Happy the sturdy, vigorous-throated bell
  Who, spite of age alert and confident,
Cries hourly, like some strong old sentinel
  Flinging the ready challenge from his tent.

For me, my soul is cracked; when, sick with care,
She strives with songs to people the cold air
  It happens often that her feeble cries

Mock the harsh rattle of a man who lies
Wounded, forgotten, 'neath a mound of slain
And dies, pinned fast, writhing his limbs in vain.

                                              (1909)

Spleen

The first and longest section of the *Fleurs du Mal* is called 'Spleen et Idéal', and very near the end of it occur four poems all bearing the same title, 'Spleen'. The word is a borrowing from English: Littré's dictionary of 1863 defines it thus:

SPLEEN (splin'), *s. m.* Nom anglais donné quelquefois à une forme de l'hypochondrie, consistant en un ennui sans cause, en un dégoût de la vie.

[English name sometimes given to a form of hypochondria, consisting of a motiveless *ennui*, a disgust with life.]

Baudelaire's *spleen* is not, therefore, an angry thing, as in 'vent one's spleen' or 'splenetic'. Rather it is a stronger and more inexplicable kind of *ennui*, a malignant boredom to which the English (so the French believed) were particularly prone. Climate and industrialization were the imagined causes. In a poem of 1852 set on a Channel steamer, Théophile Gautier writes:

> Plus pâle que le ciel livide
> Je vais au pays du charbon
> Du brouillard et du suicide;
> – Pour se tuer le temps est bon.

> [Paler than the livid sky
> I am going to the land of coal,
> of fog and of suicide.
> – It's a fine day to kill oneself.]

Baudelaire's poems, however, project no such simple solution. They speak of stagnation, artistic impotence, obsessive memories, loss of identity and of affect. In style they are among the most modern in the collection, with their urban settings, use of prosaic objects as objective correlatives for complex feelings, and irregular progression, apparently based on association of ideas rather than on logic. It is not surprising, therefore, that they have attracted some of the most ambitious and best translations of his writing.

Spleen   LXXV

Pluviôse, irrité contre la ville entière,
De son urne à grands flots verse un froid ténébreux
Aux pâles habitants du voisin cimetière
Et la mortalité sur les faubourgs brumeux.

Mon chat sur le carreau cherchant une litière
Agite sans repos son corps maigre et galeux;
L'âme d'un vieux poète erre dans la gouttière
Avec la triste voix d'un fantôme frileux.

Le bourdon se lamente, et la bûche enfumée
10 *Accompagne en fausset la pendule enrhumée,*
Cependant qu'en un jeu plein de sales parfums,

Héritage fatal d'une vieille hydropique,
Le beau valet de cœur et la dame de pique
Causent sinistrement de leurs amours défunts.

ROY FULLER

LXXV

The elements, exacerbated by
Life itself, wrap cold and sodden sheets
Round the pale people in the cemetery
And the mortality upon the streets.

Twitching at intervals his scruffy tail,
My cat's uneasy and at pains to show it;
The gutter gargles hollowly – the soul
Of some long-superannuated poet.

The sad falsetto of the smoking sticks
10   Fills in between the clock's arthritic ticks;
From an old pack, with its stale sweet perfume,

Once used to tell the fate of fat old maids,
The pretty knave of hearts, and queen of spades,
Discuss their mouldering love in tones of doom.

(1973)

Spleen   LXXVI

J'ai plus de souvenirs que si j'avais mille ans.

Un gros meuble à tiroirs encombré de bilans,
De vers, de billets doux, de procès, de romances,
Avec de lourds cheveux roulés dans des quittances,
Cache moins de secrets que mon triste cerveau.
C'est une pyramide, un immense caveau,
Qui contient plus de morts que la fosse commune.
— Je suis un cimetière abhorré de la lune,
Où comme des remords se traînent de longs vers
10   *Qui s'acharnent toujours sur mes morts les plus chers.*
Je suis un vieux boudoir plein de roses fanées,
Où gît tout un fouillis de modes surannées,
Où les pastels plaintifs et les pâles Boucher,
Seuls, respirent l'odeur d'un flacon débouché.

Rien n'égale en longueur les boiteuses journées,
Quand sous les lourds flocons des neigeuses années
L'ennui, fruit de la morne incuriosité,
Prend les proportions de l'immortalité.
— Désormais tu n'es plus, ô matière vivante!
20   *Qu'un granit entouré d'une vague épouvante,*
Assoupi dans le fond d'un Sahara brumeux;

Un vieux sphinx ignoré du monde insoucieux,
Oublié sur la carte, et dont l'humeur farouche
Ne chante qu'aux rayons du soleil qui se couche.

EDNA ST VINCENT MILLAY

The Sphinx   LXXVI

I swear to you that if I lived a thousand years
I could not be more crammed with dubious souvenirs.

There's no old chest of drawers bulging with deeds and bills,
Love-letters, locks of hair, novels, bad verses, wills,
That hides so many secrets as my wretched head; –
It's like a mausoleum, like a pyramid,
Holding more heaped unpleasant bones than Potter's Field;
I am a graveyard hated by the moon; revealed
Never by her blue light are those long worms that force
Into my dearest dead their blunt snouts of remorse.
– I am an old boudoir, where roses dried and brown
Have given their dusty odour to the faded gown,
To the ridiculous hat, doubtless in other days
So fine, among the wan pastels and pale Bouchers.

Time has gone lame, and limps; and under a thick pall
Of snow the endless years efface and muffle all;
Till boredom, fruit of the mind's inert, incurious tree,
Assumes the shape and size of immortality.
Henceforth, O living matter, you are nothing more
Than the fixed heart of chaos, soft horror's granite core,

Than a forgotten Sphinx that in some desert stands,
Drowsing beneath the heat, half-hidden by the sands,
Unmarked on any map, – whose rude and sullen frown
Lights up a moment only when the sun goes down.

(1936)

LAURENCE LERNER (1925–   )

Poet, critic and university teacher, Laurence Lerner was born and
educated in South Africa, coming to Cambridge as a graduate student
in 1945. He has published many collections of verse, as well as critical
and historical works on English literature. His translations of Baudelaire,
first published in a roneoed pamphlet by the University of Belfast, are
among the best post-1960 versions. They are often very free, but almost
always successful in rendering the feeling of a poem, sometimes by
finding convincing modern analogues for the situations and images of
the original.

Spleen I   LXXVI

I am as old as all the memories
That fill the thousand drawers behind my eyes
With old love letters, legal documents,
Verses done up in ribbon, musty scents,
Piles of receipts, and dusty locks of hair.
I am so old more secrets rot in there
Than in a thousand attics. What am I?
A cave, a pyramid, a cemetery,
Among whose corpses long worms crawl and stray,
10   Gnaw like remorse, while the moon turns away.
I am the room in which Miss Havisham
Sits brooding and remembering. I am

The roses drooping, the outmoded gowns,
The mouldy wedding cake, the croaking sounds
Of memory among the corridors
Inhabited by ghosts of buried fears.

The days go on for ever. Snow descends.
All round, the level landscape never ends,
Stretches on every side, indifferently.
20   This is a kind of immortality.
A granite Sphinx within me sits and stares
Into the desert air, vague mists of fear
Curling around its limbs. And when the long
Rays of the sunset touch its throat the air
Of the Sahara trembles with wild song.

(1967)

ROY FULLER

LXXVI

More memories than the fossils of the ages . . .

A chest of drawers stuffed with novels, pages
Of verse, love letters, writs, old balance sheets,
Forgotten curls of hair wrapped in receipts
Hides fewer secrets than my poignant skull.
That is a pyramid, a massive hull,
Rottener than mass graves of despotic states.
– I am a cemetery moonlight hates,
Where the long worm, remorse, extends its dread
And feeds on the most precious of my dead.
10   I am a boudoir full of browning blooms

Whose fashions are those of excavated tombs,
Where naive pastels and Boucher's pale style
Exude the faintness of an empty phial.

Nothing as these lame days could go as slow,
When under heavy flakes of years of snow
That offspring of incuriousness, ennui,
Stretches as long as immortality.
– O life, your truthful visage now appears!
A stone reared in the midst of unknown fears,
20   Sightless, surrounded by a Gobi's patience,
A sphinx left by the world's migrations,
White on the map, whose dotty soul cries out
Only as twilight conjures dread from doubt.

(1973)

ANTHONY HECHT (1923–)

Hecht's highly polished oeuvre has recognizable links to the cultivated, classical school of American poetry exemplified by Donald Justice or Richard Wilbur. His most noted work of translation has been Aeschylus' *Seven against Thebes*. His versions of Baudelaire find an ornate but easy-going tone that suits perfectly the alternating melancholy and world-weary ironies of the French poet.

LXXVI

I have more memories than if I had lived a thousand years.

Even a bureau crammed with souvenirs,
Old bills, love letters, photographs, receipts,
Court depositions, locks of hair in plaits,

Hides fewer secrets than my brain could yield.
It's like a tomb, a corpse-filled Potter's Field,
A pyramid where the dead lie down by scores.
I am a graveyard that the moon abhors:
Like guilty qualms, the worms burrow and nest
Thickly in bodies that I loved the best.
10 I'm a stale boudoir where old-fashioned clothes
Lie scattered among wilted fern and rose,
Where only the Boucher girls in pale pastels
Can breathe the uncorked scents and faded smells.

Nothing can equal those days for endlessness
When in the winter's blizzardy caress
Indifference expanding to Ennui
Takes on the feel of Immortality.
O living matter, henceforth you're no more
Than a cold stone encompassed by vague fear
20 And by the desert, and the mist and sun;
An ancient Sphinx ignored by everyone,
Left off the map, whose bitter irony
Is to sing as the sun sets in that dry sea.

(1961)

Spleen   LXXVII

Je suis comme le roi d'un pays pluvieux,
Riche, mais impuissant, jeune et pourtant très vieux,
Qui, de ses précepteurs méprisant les courbettes,
S'ennuie avec ses chiens comme avec d'autres bêtes.
Rien ne peut l'égayer, ni gibier, ni faucon,
Ni son peuple mourant en face du balcon.
Du bouffon favori la grotesque ballade
Ne distrait plus le front de ce cruel malade;

Son lit fleurdelisé se transforme en tombeau,
10   *Et les dames d'atour, pour qui tout prince est beau,*
Ne savent plus trouver d'impudique toilette
Pour tirer un souris de ce jeune squelette.
Le savant qui lui fait de l'or n'a jamais pu
De son être extirper l'élément corrompu,
Et dans ces bains de sang qui des Romains nous viennent,
Et dont sur leurs vieux jours les puissants se souviennent,
Il n'a su réchauffer ce cadavre hébété
Où coule au lieu de sang l'eau verte du Léthé.

LEWIS PIAGET SHANKS

Spleen   LXXVII

I'm like a king of rainy lands and cold
– wealthy, but impotent: still young, but old –
who, scornful of his tutors' bows, prefers
his hounds and boredom to such grovellers.
nor stag nor falcon rouse his apathy,
nor starving subjects 'neath his balcony.
his favourite jester's wildest ballads now
no longer clear his cruel, sickened brow;
his royal bed's a coffin drowned in care,
10   and court-ladies, to whom all kings are fair,
– seeking a smile from that young skeleton –
no longer find one shameless robe to don.
nor can the sage who makes him gold succeed
in purging him of Death's corruptive seed,

nor in the baths of blood the Romans knew,
wherein the agèd rich their strength renew,
learn how to warm that cold numb corpse, through whose
dull veins, for blood, green Lethe's waters ooze.

(1926)

ROY CAMPBELL

Spleen   LXXVII

I'm like the King of some damp, rainy clime,
Grown impotent and old before my time,
Who scorns the bows and scrapings of his teachers
And bores himself with hounds and all such creatures.
Naught can amuse him, falcon, steed, or chase:
No, not the mortal plight of his whole race
Dying before his balcony. The tune,
Sung to this tyrant by his pet buffoon,
Irks him. His couch seems far more like a grave.
Even the girls, for whom all kings seem brave,
Can think no toilet up, nor shameless rig,
To draw a smirk from this funereal prig.
The sage who makes him gold, could never find
The baser element that rots his mind.
Even those blood-baths the old Romans knew
And later thugs have imitated too,
Can't warm this skeleton to deeds of slaughter,
Whose only blood is Lethe's cold, green water.

(1952)

ROBERT LOWELL (1917–77)

The son of a prominent Boston family, Lowell was educated at Harvard and Kenyon College. His early formation was in the milieu of the New Criticism, but there is a vein of intense self-analysis in his writing which put him at the forefront of the so-called Confessional School, and which suggests an obvious, if sometimes misleading, point of comparison with Baudelaire.

His versions from *Les Fleurs du Mal* appear in *Imitations* (1961); the critical reception of these is discussed above, pp. xlv–xlviii.

Spleen   LXXVII

I'm like the king of a rain-country, rich
but sterile, young but with an old wolf's itch,
one who escapes Fénelon's apologues,
and kills the day in boredom with his dogs;
nothing cheers him, darts, tennis, falconry,
his people dying by the balcony;
the bawdry of the pet hermaphrodite
no longer gets him through a single night;
his bed of fleur-de-lys becomes a tomb;
10   even the ladies of the court, for whom
all kings are beautiful, cannot put on
shameful enough dresses for this skeleton;
the scholar who makes his gold cannot invent
washes to cleanse the poisoned element;
even in baths of blood, Rome's legacy,
our tyrants' solace in senility,
he cannot warm up his shot corpse, whose food
is syrup-green Lethean ooze, not blood.

(1961)

NICHOLAS MOORE (1918–86)

Poet and horticulturalist, Moore was the son of the philosopher G. E. Moore and nephew of the poet Thomas Sturge Moore, also featured in this volume. Nine collections of his poetry appeared between 1941 and 1950. Then, to quote his autobiographical note, he 'engaged unprofitably in various forms of horticulture (including writing a now out-of-date book on the tall bearded iris)' until in 1964 he 'became ill with a gangrened foot and was found to have diabetes'. He began to write again in 1967, and in 1968 when the *Sunday Times*, as a competition, invited translations of 'Je suis comme le roi . . .' (to be judged by George Steiner), he submitted no fewer than thirty-one entries, under a variety of sardonic pseudonyms and from addresses, mostly fictitious, in this country and abroad. The nearest equivalent to this *tour de force* is perhaps Raymond Queneau's *Exercices de style*. The versions were published under the title *Spleen* and with an essay by Moore 'On the Impossibility of Translation' by the Menard Press in 1973, and reprinted by them in 1990.

The Islets of Langerhans are patches of endocrine tissue in the pancreas. Their failure to produce insulin is the cause of diabetes.

On the Islets of Langerhans   LXXVII
(KING MIDAS IN REVERSE)
(for Nicholas Moore)

I'm like the monarch of a damp, cold islet,
Live, but cut-off; young still, but, when I smile, it
Hurts almost, and my doctors' precepts irk me.
I'm bored with living things. Nothing can jerk me
Out of this sluggish gloom, nor sport, nor plaything.
My family's decline is not a gay thing.
Lenny's sick jokes; the ballads of Jacques Brel
Don't quite, in face of this cruel sickness, jell.

My bedroom iris, scrawled on Thotmes' tomb,
10   Is deadly as the fat dames who presume –
Worshipping princes – to disclose their wares
Quite nakedly – but bore this corpse to tears.
The Income-Tax Repayment in the bank
Can't win from this too-sugared heart one thank
You, nor the bloody slaughter in Vietnam
Raise in my diabetic bones one damn
Of youthful fire; my frozen limbs turn green –
Where flows not blood, but Lethe – with gangrene.

> *Conilho Moraes*
> c/o The PBS,
> 4 St James' Square,
> SW1

(1968)

After the Deluge   LXXVII
(for Letty, Lys and Fleur – those undying graces)

Not riches, power, advisers, pets, sport, gold
Nor even naked women cheer the old
In heart. Bones will be bones. All that remains
Instead of blood, green water, clotted veins.

> *C. H. Bare: Ire*
> Art C.,
> Pic.,
> W1

(1968)

LAURENCE LERNER

Spleen II   LXXVII

It rains all year in the oppressive land
Of which I am the young decrepit king.
My tutors bow and scrape on every hand;
I much prefer my dogs; but dogs no more
Than stag or falcon, horse or anything
Amuse me now. My favourite dwarf can sing
Grotesque and filthy songs, I pay no heed.
My people die in herds around my door:
I do not care; I'm sick: on my huge bed,
Half smothered by the hanging fleurs-de-lys,
I lie all day imagining I'm dead.

My harlots peel off stockings, show black lace,
Let the last garment linger: not a smile
Plays on the skull that serves me for a face.

I keep an alchemist: his subtle art
Can purify, refine, turn lead to gold,
But cannot purge the dross that clogs my heart.

I've even thought of killings, Roman style,
(One thinks about such things as one grows old);
But if my streets ran blood, and all the drains
Were gushing blood, it wouldn't thaw the cold
And frozen muck of Lethe in my veins.

(1967)

Spleen   LXXVIII

Quand le ciel bas et lourd pèse comme un couvercle
Sur l'esprit gémissant en proie aux longs ennuis,
Et que de l'horizon embrassant tout le cercle
Il nous verse un jour noir plus triste que les nuits;

Quand la terre est changée en un cachot humide,
Où l'Espérance, comme une chauve-souris,
S'en va battant les murs de son aile timide
Et se cognant la tête à des plafonds pourris;

Quand la pluie étalant ses immenses traînées
10   D'une vaste prison imite les barreaux,
Et qu'un peuple muet d'infâmes araignées
Vient tendre ses filets au fond de nos cerveaux,

Des cloches tout à coup sautent avec furie
Et lancent vers le ciel un affreux hurlement,
Ainsi que des esprits errants et sans patrie
Qui se mettent à geindre opiniâtrement.

— Et de longs corbillards, sans tambours ni musique,
Défilent lentement dans mon âme; l'Espoir,
Vaincu, pleure, et l'Angoisse atroce, despotique,
20   Sur mon crâne incliné plante son drapeau noir.

H. C.

Dejection   LXXVIII

When, as a lid, the low and heavy sky
Weighs down the soul that long misfortunes blight,
And all the horizon, far as meets the eye,
Shows a black day, more gloomy than the night,

When earth is changed into a cold damp jail,
Where hope, like some poor bat, within it fled,
Does with its frightened wing the walls assail,
And 'gainst the rotten ceiling strike its head.

When falling in long streaming lines the rain,
Vast prison bars before our fancy sets,
And hosts of loathsome spiders o'er our brain
Come silently, and weave and spread their nets.

Bells of a sudden fiercely clash, and fling
A frightful clamour to the startled sky,
Like exiled spirits, homeless, wandering,
Who utter groans and shrieks incessantly.

Long hearses without drums or psalmody,
March slowly through my soul – Hope, conquered quite,
Weeps – and despotic, cruel Agony,
O'er my bowed head plants its flag black as night.

(1894)

J. C. SQUIRE

Spleen   LXXVIII

When the low heavy sky weighs like a lid
    Upon the spirit aching for the light,
And all the wide horizon's line is hid
    By a black day sadder than any night;

When the changed earth is but a dungeon dank
    Where batlike Hope goes blindly fluttering
And, striking wall and roof and mouldering plank,
    Bruises his tender head and timid wing;

When like grim prison-bars stretch down the thin,
10   Straight, rigid pillars of the endless rain,
And the dumb throngs of infamous spiders spin
    Their meshes in the caverns of the brain; –

Suddenly, bells leap forth into the air,
    Hurling a hideous uproar to the sky
As 'twere a band of homeless spirits who fare
    Through the strange heavens, wailing stubbornly.

And hearses, without drum or instrument,
    File slowly through my soul; crushed, sorrowful,
Weeps Hope, and Grief, fierce and omnipotent,
20   Plants his black banner on my drooping skull.

(1909)

LAURENCE LERNER

Spleen III   LXXVIII

When the low sky hangs heavy as a lid,
Pressing like boredom on our baffled sight,
Seals the horizon and lets down a flood
Of daylight, sadder, filthier than night;

When earth becomes a dungeon, shutting in
Hope like a bat that darts and twists and falls,
Scraping the roof with head or timid wing,
Dislodging plaster from the rotten walls;

When the interminable lines of rain
10 Are stretched like prison bars before our sight,
And a mute horde of spiders in the brain
Wrap their disgusting webs round every thought

Bells lose their temper suddenly; leap high,
Screaming like ghosts, homeless and obstinate,
Flinging their furious noises at the sky.
No land no language owns the sounds they made

No drum, no music sounds; in the still air
Black hearses slowly move across the soul.
Hope weeps, defeated; and, see, King Despair
20 Plants his black flag upon the slopes of skull.

(1967)

ROY FULLER

LXXVIII

When, a great manhole lid, the heavy sky
Falls and fits neatly on the horizon's ring
And on the spirit, bored with misery;
The day dark, sadder than an evening;

When earth is changed into an oozing cell
Where, like a bat in daylight, Hope's frail wing
Is bruised against the walls, its little skull
Beating and beating on the leprous ceiling;

When, as the bars of an enormous jail,
10   Spread and descend the verticals of rain,
And a silent race of noisome spiders trail
Their similar filaments inside one's brain,

A terrible shouting rises to the sky –
The sudden furious clappers of the bells –
Like the beginning of that endless cry
Of souls condemned to temporary hells.

– And long cortèges, with neither drums nor trumpets,
File slowly through my being; beaten Hope
Weeps, and the atrocious tyrant, Anguish, sets
20   His sable banner on my outstretched nape.

(1973)

ROY CAMPBELL

Obsession   LXXIX

You forests, like cathedrals, are my dread:
You roar like organs. Our curst hearts, like cells
Where death forever rattles on the bed,
Echo your *de Profundis* as it swells.

My spirit hates you, Ocean! sees, and loathes
Its tumults in your own. Of men defeated
The bitter laugh, that's full of sobs and oaths,
Is in your own tremendously repeated.

How you would please me, Night! without your stars
10 Which speak a foreign dialect, that jars
On one who seeks the void, the black, the bare.

Yet even your darkest shade a canvas forms
Whereupon my eye must multiply in swarms
Familiar looks of shapes no longer there.

(1952)

The Thirst for the Void   LXXX

My soul, you used to love the battle's rumble.
Hope, whose sharp spur once kindled you like flame,
Will mount on you no more. Rest, without shame,
Old charger, since at every step you stumble.

Sleep now the sleep of brutes, proud heart: be humble.

O broken raider, for your outworn mettle,
Love has no joys, no fight is worth disputing.
Farewell to all the trumpeting and fluting!
Pleasure, have done, when brooding shadows settle,

10   The blooms of spring are vanquished by the nettle.

As snows devour stiff corpses in their welter,
Time wolfs my soul in, minute after minute.
I've seen the world and everything that's in it,
And I no longer seek in it for shelter;

Come, Avalanche! and sweep me helter-skelter.

(1952)

JAMES MCGOWAN

The Taste for Nothingness   LXXX

Dull soul, to whom the battle once was sweet,
Hope, who had spurred your ardour and your fame
Will no more ride you! Lie down without shame
Old horse, who makes his way on stumbling feet.

Give up, my heart, and sleep your stolid sleep.

For you old rover, spirit sadly spent,
Love is no longer fair, nor is dispute;
Farewell to brass alarms, sighs of the flute!
Pleasures, give up a heart grown impotent!

10   The Spring, once wonderful, has lost its scent!

And Time engulfs me in its steady tide,
As blizzards cover corpses with their snow;
And poised on high I watch the world below,
No longer looking for a place to hide.

Avalanche, sweep me off within your slide!

(1993)

Alchemy of Suffering   LXXXI

One's ardour, Nature, makes you bright,
One finds within you mourning, grief!
What speaks to one of tombs and death
Says to the other, Splendour! Life!

Mystical Hermes, help to me,
Intimidating though you are,
You make me Midas' counterpart,
No sadder alchemist than he;

My gold is iron by your spell,
And paradise turns into hell;
I see in winding-sheets of clouds

A dear cadaver in its shroud,
And there upon celestial strands
I raise huge tombs above the sands.

(1993)

ROY CAMPBELL

Sympathetic Horror   LXXXII

From livid skies that, without end,
As stormy as your future roll,
What thoughts into your empty soul
(Answer me, libertine!) descend?

– Insatiable yet for all
That turns on darkness, doom, or dice,
I'll not, like Ovid, mourn my fall,
Chased from the Latin paradise.

Skies, torn like seacoasts by the storm!
10   In you I see my pride take form,
And the huge clouds that rush in streams

Are the black hearses of my dreams,
And your red rays reflect the hell,
In which my heart is pleased to dwell.

(1952)

The Irremediable   LXXXIV

i

A Form, Idea, or Essence, chased
Out of the azure sky, and shot
Into a leaden Styx where not
A star can pierce the muddy waste:

An angel, rash explorer, who,
Tempted by love of strange deformity,
Caught in a nightmare of enormity,
Fights like a swimmer, wrestling through

A monstrous whorl of eddying spume,
In deathly anguish, from him flinging
The wave that, like an idiot singing,
Goes pirouetting through the gloom:

A wretch enchanted, who, to flee
A den of serpents, gropes about
In desperation vain, without
Discovering a match or key:

A damnèd soul, who, with no lamp,
Stands by a gulf, whose humid scent
Betrays the depth of the descent
Of endless stairs without a ramp,

Where slimy monsters watch the track
Whose eyeballs phosphoresce and glow
Only to make the night more black
And nought except themselves to show:

A vessel that the pole betrays,
Caught in a crystal trap all round,
And seeking by what fatal sound
It ever entered such a maze: —

Clear emblems! measuring the level
30   Of irremediable dooms,
Which make us see how well the Devil
Performs whatever he presumes!

ii

Strange *tête-à-tête!* the heart, its own
Mirror, its own confession hears!
Deep well where Truth is trembling shown
And like a livid star appears,

Ironic beacon and infernal
Torch of satanic grace, but still
Sole glory and relief eternal,
40   — Conscience that operates in Ill!

(1952)

Tableaux Parisiens

Parisian Pictures

JOHN ASHBERY (1927–   )

Having studied French literature as a postgraduate at Columbia and New York University and worked in publishing for four years (during which time he wrote his two first collections of poetry), Ashbery spent seven years in France as an art critic and foreign correspondent before returning to New York, where he edited *Art News* and produced numerous volumes of verse. This translation of 'Paysage' – his only version of Baudelaire – comes from *A Wave* (1984).

Line 21 translates '*L'Emeute, tempêtant vainement à ma vitre*'; 'l'Emeute' (Riot), with its capital letter, is usually taken to refer to the political disturbances of 1848 and 1851. Compare Lerner's rendering.

Landscape   LXXXVI
(after Baudelaire)

I want a bedroom near the sky, an astrologer's cave
Where I can fashion eclogues that are chaste and grave.
Dreaming, I'll hear the wind in the steeples close by
Sweep the solemn hymns away. I'll spy
On factories from my attic window, resting my chin
In both hands, drinking in the songs, the din.
I'll see chimneys and steeples, those masts of the city,
And the huge sky that makes us dream of eternity.

How sweet to watch the birth of the star in the still-blue
10 Sky, through mist; the lamp burning anew
At the window; rivers of coal climbing the firmament
And the moon pouring out its pale enchantment.
I'll see the spring, the summer and the fall
And when winter casts its monotonous pall
Of snow, I'll draw the blinds and curtains tight
And build my magic palaces in the night;

Then dream of gardens, of bluish horizons,
Of jets of water weeping in alabaster basins,
Of kisses, of birds singing at dawn and at nightfall,
20   Of all that's most childish in our pastoral.
When the storm rattles my windowpane
I'll stay hunched at my desk, it will roar in vain
For I'll have plunged deep inside the thrill
Of conjuring spring with the force of my will,
Coaxing the sun from my heart, and building here
Out of my fiery thoughts, a tepid atmosphere.

(1984)

LAURENCE LERNER

Landscape   LXXXVI

I need to live among the roofs and towers
Like an astrologer among his stars,
I need to dream (to write my pastorals)
Through solemn noises from the nearby bells,
And wake, and hear them still: lean out and see
The many-masted city under me,
Paris, my restless workshop: drainpipes, spires:
The endless sky in reach of my desires.

Windows and stars light up among the mist.
10   I lean and watch, my chin upon my fist.
Rivers of smoke ascend and merge; the pale
And blatant moon is pouring out her spell.

Year in year out I'll watch the seasons pass
– Spring, summer, autumn – staring through the glass,
Till winter spreads its white monotony
Then close the shutters on my fantasy.

All night in dreams I'll pass through shimmering halls;
Fountains will weep from alabaster bowls.
Birds sing and lovers kiss beneath blue skies,
20   The sound of flutes makes palaces arise.
Winter can riot at the window pane,
I shall not lift my head, or hear the rain.
Drowned in the damp voluptuous atmosphere
Through which my childhood idylls reappear,
In which the sun that sets my thoughts on fire
Charges the heavy climate with desire.

(1967)

ANTHONY RYLE (1927–   )

Anthony Ryle was educated at University College, Oxford, and has
now retired from a career as a psychotherapist. Neither this translation
nor no. CIII has been previously published.

The Sun   LXXXVII

At the edge of the town the houses hide
Their secret vices behind blinds; outside
The sun assaults with a redoubled heat
City and meadow, rooftops, fields of wheat.

Fencing in fantasy, I make this my time
To flush, from each dark corner, a chance rhyme,
Words trip me up like paving stones and throw
Whole poems at me, dreamed of long ago.

This foster-father sun at once disposes
Of pallor and wakes up, with verse and roses,
The fields, turns doubt to vapour and contrives
To fill with sweetness both our minds and hives;
He gives youth back to cripples and imparts
The gaiety of young girls to their hearts;
He sees that crops grow to maturity
In fertile hearts seeking immortality.

He comes to our towns like a poet, transforming
Their utmost corruption, and, like a king,
But without any servants or pomp, he calls
On all the palaces, all the hospitals.

(1995)

RICHARD HOWARD

To a Red-haired Beggar Girl   LXXXVIII

Gaping tatters in each garment prove
your calling is not only beggary
   but beauty as well.

and to a poet equally 'reduced',
the frail and freckled body you display
   makes its own appeal –

queens in velvet buskins take the stage
less regally than you wade through the mud
   on your wooden clogs.

10 What if, instead of these indecent rags,
the splendid train of a brocaded gown
   rustled at your heels,

and rather than town stockings, just suppose
curious glances sliding up your thigh
   met with a gold dirk!

And then if, for our sins, those flimsy knots
released two perfect little breasts that shine
   brighter than your eyes,

and your own arms consented to reveal
20 the rest, though archly feigning to fend off
   hands that go too far . . .

Strands of pearls and strophes by Belleau
arriving in – imagine! – endless streams
   'from an admirer';

riffraff – talented and otherwise –
offering tributes to the slippered feet
   glimpsed from below stairs;

gentlemen sending flunkeys to find out
who owns the carriage always told to 'wait'
30   at your smart address

where, in the boudoir, kisses count for more
than quarterings, although the cast includes
   a Bourbon or two!

– Meanwhile, here you are, begging scraps
doled out by the local *table d'hôte*
   at the kitchen door

and scavenging discarded finery
worth forty sous, a price which (pardon me!)
   I cannot afford . . .

40   Go, then, my Beauty, with no ornament
   – patchouli or pearl choker – but your own
     starveling nakedness!

(1982)

Le Cygne

This poem, now regarded as one of Baudelaire's greatest, was rejected
when he first offered it for publication in 1859. The location is the
Place du Carrousel, which was created in 1852 by demolishing several
streets of old houses in which artists and poets had formerly lived. Victor
Hugo was himself living in political exile on Guernsey at the time of
the dedication. The '*Simoïs menteur*' of line 4 is a free translation of
Virgil's '*falsi Simoentis ad undam*', Aeneid III, 302.

Le Cygne   LXXXIX
A Victor Hugo

i

Andromaque, je pense à vous! Ce petit fleuve,
Pauvre et triste miroir où jadis resplendit
L'immense majesté de vos douleurs de veuve,
Ce Simoïs menteur qui par vos pleurs grandit,

A fécondé soudain ma mémoire fertile,
Comme je traversais le nouveau Carrousel.
Le vieux Paris n'est plus (la forme d'une ville
Change plus vite, hélas! que le cœur d'un mortel);

Je ne vois qu'en esprit tout ce camp de baraques,
10   Ces tas de chapiteaux ébauchés et de fûts,
Les herbes, les gros blocs verdis par l'eau des flaques,
Et, brillant aux carreaux, le bric-à-brac confus.

Là s'étalait jadis une ménagerie;
Là je vis, un matin, à l'heure où sous les cieux
Froids et clairs le Travail s'éveille, où la voirie
Pousse un sombre ouragan dans l'air silencieux,

Un cygne qui s'était évadé de sa cage,
Et, de ses pieds palmés frottant le pavé sec,
Sur le sol raboteux traînait son blanc plumage.
20   Près d'un ruisseau sans eau la bête ouvrant le bec

Baignait nerveusement ses ailes dans la poudre,
Et disait, le cœur plein de son beau lac natal:
«Eau, quand donc pleuvras-tu? quand tonneras-tu, foudre?»
Je vois ce malheureux, mythe étrange et fatal,

Vers le ciel quelquefois, comme l'homme d'Ovide,
Vers le ciel ironique et cruellement bleu,
Sur son cou convulsif tendant sa tête avide,
Comme s'il adressait des reproches à Dieu!

ii

Paris change! mais rien dans ma mélancolie
30   N'a bougé! palais neufs, échafaudages, blocs,
Vieux faubourgs, tout pour moi devient allégorie,
Et mes chers souvenirs sont plus lourds que des rocs.

Aussi devant ce Louvre une image m'opprime:
Je pense à mon grand cygne, avec ses gestes fous,
Comme les exilés, ridicule et sublime,
Et rongé d'un désir sans trêve! et puis à vous,

Andromaque, des bras d'un grand époux tombée,
Vil bétail, sous la main du superbe Pyrrhus,
Auprès d'un tombeau vide en extase courbée;
40   Veuve d'Hector, hélas! et femme d'Hélénus!

Je pense à la négresse, amaigrie et phtisique,
Piétinant dans la boue, et cherchant, l'œil hagard,
Les cocotiers absents de la superbe Afrique
Derrière la muraille immense du brouillard;

A quiconque a perdu ce qui ne se retrouve
Jamais, jamais! à ceux qui s'abreuvent de pleurs
Et tettent la Douleur comme une bonne louve!
Aux maigres orphelins séchant comme des fleurs!

Ainsi dans la forêt où mon esprit s'exile
50   Un vieux Souvenir sonne à plein souffle du cor!
Je pense aux matelots oubliés dans une île,
Aux captifs, aux vaincus! . . . à bien d'autres encor!

F. P. STURM

The Swan   LXXXIX
To Victor Hugo

i

Andromache, I think of you! The stream,
The poor, sad mirror where in bygone days
Shone all the majesty of your widowed grief,
The lying Simoïs flooded by your tears,
Made all my fertile memory blossom forth
As I passed by the new-built Carrousel.
Old Paris is no more (a town, alas,
Changes more quickly than man's heart may change);
Yet in my mind I still can see the booths;
The heaps of brick and rough-hewn capitals;
The grass; the stones all over-green with moss;
The débris, and the square-set heaps of tiles.

There a menagerie was once outspread;
And there I saw, one morning at the hour
When Toil awakes beneath the cold, clear sky,
And the road roars upon the silent air,

A swan who had escaped his cage, and walked
On the dry pavement with his webby feet,
And trailed his spotless plumage on the ground.
And near a waterless stream the piteous swan
Opened his beak, and bathing in the dust
His nervous wings, he cried (his heart the while
Filled with a vision of his own fair lake):

'O water, when then wilt thou come in rain?
Lightning, when wilt thou glitter?'
                                    Sometimes yet
I see the hapless bird – strange, fatal myth –
Like him that Ovid writes of, lifting up
Unto the cruelly blue, ironic heavens,
30   With stretched, convulsive neck a thirsty face,
As though he sent reproaches up to God!

ii

Paris may change; my melancholy is fixed.
New palaces, and scaffoldings, and blocks,
And suburbs old, are symbols all to me
Whose memories are as heavy as a stone.
And so, before the Louvre, to vex my soul,
The image came of my majestic swan
With his made gestures, foolish and sublime,
As of an exile whom one great desire
40   Gnaws with no truce. And then I thought of you,
Andromache! torn from your hero's arms;
Beneath the hand of Pyrrhus in his pride;
Bent o'er an empty tomb in ecstasy;
Widow of Hector – wife of Helenus!
And of the Negress, wan and phthisical,
Tramping the mud, and with her haggard eyes
Seeking beyond the mighty walls of fog
The absent palm-trees of proud Africa;
Of all who lose that which they never find;
50   Of all who drink of tears; all whom grey Grief
Gives suck to as the kindly wolf gave suck;
Of meagre orphans who like blossoms fade.

And one old Memory like a crying horn
Sounds through the forest where my soul is lost . . .
I think of sailors on some isle, forgotten;
Of captives, vanquished . . . and of many more.

(1906)

ANTHONY HECHT

The Swan   LXXXIX

i

Andromache, I think of you. The little stream,
A yellowing mirror that onetime beheld
The huge solemnity of your widow's grief,
(This deceiving Simois that your tears have swelled)

Suddenly flooded the memory's dark soil
As I was crossing the *Place du Carrousel*.
The old Paris is gone (the face of a town
Is more changeable than the heart of mortal man).

I see what seem the ghosts of these royal barracks,
10   The rough-hewn capitals, the columns waiting to crack,
Weeds, and the big rocks greened with standing water,
And at the window, Their Majesty's bric-a-brac.

One time a menagerie was on display there,
And there I saw one morning at the hour
Of cold and clarity when Labor rises
And brooms make little cyclones of soot in the air

A swan that had escaped out of his cage,
And there, web-footed on the dry sidewalk,
Dragged his white plumes over the cobblestones,
20   Lifting his beak at the gutter as if to talk,

And bathing his wings in the sifting city dust,
His heart full of some cool, remembered lake,
Said, 'Water, when will you rain? Where is your thunder?'
I can see him now, straining his twitching neck

Skyward again and again, like the man in Ovid,
Toward an ironic heaven as blank as slate,
And trapped in a ruinous myth, he lifts his head
As if God were the object of his hate.

ii

Paris changes, but nothing of my melancholy
30   Gives way. Foundations, scaffoldings, tackle and blocks,
And the old suburbs drift off into allegory,
While my frailest memories take on the weight of rocks.

And so at the Louvre one image weighs me down:
I think of my great swan, the imbecile strain
Of his head, noble and foolish as all the exiled,
Eaten by ceaseless needs – and once again

Of you, Andromache, from a great husband's arms
Fallen to the whip and mounted lust of Pyrrhus,
And slumped in a heap beside an empty tomb,
40   (Poor widow of Hector, and bride of Helenus)

And think of the consumptive negress, stamping
In mud, emaciate, and trying to see
The vanished coconuts of hidden Africa
Behind the thickening granite of the mist;

Of whoever has lost what cannot be found again,
Ever, ever; of those who lap up the tears
And nurse at the teats of that motherly she-wolf, Sorrow;
Of orphans drying like flowers in empty jars.

So in that forest where my mind is exiled
50   One memory sounds like brass in the ancient war:
I think of sailors washed up on uncharted islands,
Of prisoners, the conquered, and more, so many more.

(1961)

JOHN GOUDGE

The Seven Old Men   XC

City swarming with people! City crowded with dreams!
Through the narrow back streets of this mighty colossus,
Like the sap in a tree, a dark mystery streams,
And ghosts clutch a man's sleeve, in broad day, as he passes.

One morning when the houses that lined the sad street
Hovered larger than life, so it seemed, in the mist,
And resembled the banks of a river in spate,
A stage set for the shade of a pantomimist,

In the foul, yellow fog that pervaded the whole
10   Atmosphere I strode on, like a hero in battle,
Each nerve taut, and communed with my world-weary soul,
While the carts made the neighbourhood shake with their
        rattle.

All at once in the gloom, an old man came in sight,
Wearing tatters as yellow as thundery skies,
And a torrent of alms had showered down at his plight,
Were it not for the malice that gleamed in his eyes,

You'd have said that his beard was as long as a lance,
Jutting out, and the equal of Judas' quite,
That his eyeballs were floating in bile, that his glance
20 Was so cold as to sharpen the sting of frostbite.

He was not so much crooked as broken, his spine
With his legs represented a perfect right-angle,
And his stick put the finishing touch to his mien,
For it gave him the gait of and made him resemble

A lame four-footed beast or a jew with three legs.
'Twas as though in the mud and the snow as he went,
He was trampling the dead underground with his clogs –
Rather hateful and spiteful than indifferent.

His twin followed him close, beard, back, stick, rags and eye,
30 By no mark could you tell one foul fiend from his brother.
These grotesque apparitions, pace for pace, went their way,
Each was bound for the same unknown end as the other.

Was it wicked mischance that had made me a fool?
By some infamous plot was I being seduced?
I know not, but I counted this sinister ghoul
Seven times in seven minutes, by himself reproduced.

And the man who makes fun of my disquietude
And who feels not the chill of a brotherly shiver
Should mark well that despite such decrepitude
40 These grim brutes had the look of surviving for ever.

Had an eighth then appeared, I believe I'd have died –
One more pitiless twin sent to menace and mock,
An incestuous phoenix, by himself multiplied –
But I took to my heels and presented my back

To this ghastly parade. As if drunk, vision doubled,
Panic-struck, I ran home, shut the door, turned the key;
I was ill, overcome, hot and cold, deeply troubled,
At once baffled and hurt by the absurdity.

And in vain did my reason attempt to take charge,
50   For its efforts were foiled by the tempest in me,
And my soul began dancing a jig, like a barge
Without masts on a monstrous and infinite sea.

(1979)

ROY CAMPBELL

The Little Old Women   XCI
To Victor Hugo

i

In sinuous folds of cities old and grim,
Where all things, even horror, turn to grace,
I follow, in obedience to my whim,
Strange, feeble, charming creatures round the place.

These crooked freaks were women in their pride,
Fair Eponine or Laïs! Humped and bent,
Love them! Because they still have souls inside.
Under their draughty skirts in tatters rent,

They crawl: a vicious wind their carrion rides;
10   From the deep roar of traffic see them cower,
Pressing like precious relics to their sides
Some satchel stitched with mottoes or a flower.

They trot like marionettes along the level,
Or drag themselves like wounded deer, poor crones!
Or dance, against their will, as if the devil
Were swinging in the belfry of their bones.

Cracked though they are, their eyes are sharp as drills
And shine, like pools of water in the night, –
The eyes of little girls whom wonder thrills
20   To laugh at all that sparkles and is bright.

The coffins of old women very often
Are near as small as those of children are.
Wise Death, who makes a symbol of a coffin
Displays a taste both charming and bizarre.

And when I track some feeble phantom fleeing
Through Paris's immense ant-swarming Babel,
I always think that such a fragile being
Is moving softly to another cradle.

Unless, sometimes, in geometric mood,
30   To see the strange deformities they offer,
I muse how often he who saws the wood
Must change the shape and outline of the coffer.

Those eyes are wells a million teardrops feed,
Crucibles spangled by a cooling ore,
Invincible in charm to all that breed
Austere Misfortune suckled with her lore.

ii

Vestal whom old Frascati could enamour:
Thalia's nun, whose name was only known
To her dead prompter: madcap full of glamour
40   Whom Tivoli once sheltered as its own –

They all elate me. But of these a few,
Of sorrow having made a honeyed leaven,
Say to Devotion, 'Lend me wings anew,
O powerful Hippogriff, and fly to heaven.'

One for her fatherland a martyr: one
By her own husband wronged beyond belief:
And one a pierced Madonna through her son –
They all could make a river with their grief.

iii

Yes, I have followed them, time and again!
50   One, I recall, when sunset, like a heart,
Bled through the sky from wounds of ruddy stain,
Pensively sat upon a seat apart,

To listen to the music, rich in metal,
That's played by bands of soldiers in the parks
On golden, soul-reviving eves, to fettle,
From meek civilian hearts, heroic sparks.

This one was straight and stiff, in carriage regal,
She breathed the warrior-music through her teeth,
Opened her eye like that of an old eagle,
60   And bared a forehead moulded for a wreath.

iv

Thus, then, you journey, uncomplaining, stoic
Across the strife of modern cities flung,
Sad mothers, courtesans, or saints heroic,
Whose names of old were heard on every tongue,

You once were grace, and you were glory once.
None know you now. Derisory advances
Some drunkard makes you, mixed with worse affronts.
And on your heels a child-tormentor prances.

But I who watch you tenderly: and measure
70   With anxious eye, your weak unsteady gait
As would a father – get a secret pleasure
On your account, as on your steps I wait.

I see your passionate and virgin crazes;
Sombre or bright, I see your vanished prime;
My soul, resplendent with your virtue, blazes,
And revels in your vices and your crimes.

Poor wrecks! My family! Kindred in mind, you
Receive from me every day my last addresses.
Eighty-year Eves, will yet tomorrow find you
80   On whom the claw of God so fiercely presses?

(1952)

THOMAS STURGE MOORE
(1870–1944)

English poet and wood-engraver, he was the brother of the philosopher
G. E. Moore and uncle of the poet Nicholas Moore. He was a friend
of W. B. Yeats and produced designs for several of his books. He
wrote several verse plays and a large body of poetry, including four
translations from Baudelaire.

The Blind   XCII

Consider them, my soul, how horrible!
Like draper's dummies vaguely ludicrous;
Singular as somnambulists; still thus
Rolling vain eyeballs, wherefore? who can tell?
Do pupils whence the spark divine has fled
Yet long to scan afar and, ill at ease,
Probe upward? Never o'er the pavement these
In pensive reverie droop the full-charged head.
They ford across an endless black abyss
10 That brother is to silence. Hear they this
City around them laugh and howl, and grind
At pleasure as at some atrocious task?
I too drag on, more stultified I ask:
What can we seek in Heaven, all we blind?

(1932)

Le Squelette Laboureur

This is one of a small number of poems in which Baudelaire takes a pre-existing art work and creatively misreads it, either identifying with the main figure (as in 'Les Plaintes d'un Icare' [XII]), 'overhearing' it ('L'Amour et le Crâne', CXVII), or as here, questioning it and supplying his own replies. The source here is an anatomical plate, probably from Vesalius's *Humani corporis fabrica* (1543). The skeleton and *écorché* are digging so as to demonstrate the movement of the long bones and play of the muscles: the terrifying message about the afterlife is entirely Baudelaire's own invention.

Le Squelette Laboureur   XCIV

i

> Dans les planches d'anatomie
> Qui traînent sur ces quais poudreux
> Où maint livre cadavéreux
> Dort comme une antique momie,
>
> Dessins auxquels la gravité
> Et le savoir d'un vieil artiste,
> Bien que le sujet en soit triste,
> Ont communiqué la Beauté,
>
> On voit, ce qui rend plus complètes
> Ces mystérieuses horreurs,
> Bêchant comme des laboureurs,
> Des Ecorchés et des Squelettes.

10

ii

De ce terrain que vous fouillez,
Manants résignés et funèbres,
De tout l'effort de vos vertèbres,
Ou de vos muscles dépouillés,

Dites, quelle moisson étrange,
Forçats arrachés au charnier,
Tirez-vous, et de quel fermier
20 Avez-vous à remplir la grange?

Voulez-vous (d'un destin trop dur
Epouvantable et clair emblème!)
Montrer que dans la fosse même
Le sommeil promis n'est pas sûr;

Qu'envers nous le Néant est traître;
Que tout, même la Mort, nous ment,
Et que sempiternellement,
Hélas! il nous faudra peut-être

Dans quelque pays inconnu
30 Ecorcher la terre revêche
Et pousser une lourde bêche
Sous notre pied sanglant et nu?

LEWIS PIAGET SHANKS

Le Squelette Laboureur   XCIV

i

in anatomic charts, upon
the parapets of dusty quays,
where coffined volumes lie at peace
like mummies dozing in the sun,

– drawings wherein the solemn zeal
of dexterous hands long turned to dust,
in things of sadness or disgust
have shown the beauty of the real –

we find – and then these lexicons
10 of cryptic horror grow complete! –
spading, like farmers, with their feet,
cadavers flayed and skeletons.

ii

say, from the earth ye ransack there,
o patients serfs funereal,
with all your straining backbones, all
the strength of muscles peeled and bare,

tell me, o galley-slaves who moil,
from graves and charnel-houses torn,
whose barn ye hope to fill? what corn
20 will crown your long mysterious toil?

would ye (a proof in miniature
of some intolerable doom!)
teach us that even in the tomb
our promised sleep is not secure;

that graves, like all things else, are traps,
and nothingness another lie;
and that, although we mortals die,
'twill be our fate at last, perhaps,

in lands of loneliness complete,
30   to dig some rocky counterscarp,
pushing a heavy spade and sharp
beneath our naked bleeding feet?

(1926)

ROY CAMPBELL

There is a more faithful rendering of 'Le Squelette Laboureur' in
Campbell's complete translation, but this early and very free version
incorporates reminiscences of 'Danse Macabre' (XCVII) to striking
effect.

Overtime   XCIV

Amongst the ponderous tomes of learning,
Dull texts of medicine and law,
With idle thumb the pages turning
In sudden carnival, I saw,

Revelling forth into the day
In scarlet liveries, nine or ten
Survivors of their own decay –
The flayed anatomies of men:
And marked how well the scalpel's care
10 Was aided by the painter's tones
To liven with a jaunty air
Their crazy trellises of bones.
In regimental stripes and bands
Each emphasised the cause he serves –
Here was a grenadier of glands
And there a gay hussar of nerves:
And one his skin peeled off as though
A workman's coat with surly shrug
The flexion of the thews to show,
20 Treading a shovel, grimly dug.
Dour sexton, working overtime,
With gristly toes he hooked his spade
To trench the very marl and slime
In which he should have long been laid.
The lucky many of the dead –
Their suit of darkness fits them tight,
Buttoned with stars from foot to head
They wear the uniform of Night;
But some for extra shift are due
30 Who, slaves for any fool to blame,
With a flayed sole the ages through
Must push the shovel of their fame.

(1933)

SEAMUS HEANEY (1939–)

The Irish poet and critic was educated at Queen's University, Belfast. His recent poetry, drawing on the experience of his acute and wide-ranging critical activity, displays a broadening of reference into the literary sphere. He was Oxford Professor of Poetry from 1989 to 1994, and was awarded the Nobel Prize for Literature in 1995.

At first glance a poet whose natural territory is far removed from that of Baudelaire, none the less Heaney found in 'Le Squelette Laboureur' a fortuitous convergence of subject-matter with his own poems about the bodies of sacrificial victims preserved in peat-bogs. 'The Digging Skeleton' fits into this cycle (in *North*) as a dark meditation on the eternal nature of suffering. Heaney's translation, rather free in its details, assimilates the poem to the topography of its new context ('red slobland' and 'muscles like plaited sedge', images without equivalents in the original, echo the terrain of the bog poems; 'navvies' and 'death's lifers' evoke more recent Irish history) while remaining faithful to the outline of Baudelaire's nightmarish conceit.

The Digging Skeleton   XCIV
after Baudelaire

i

You find anatomical plates
Buried along these dusty quays
Among books yellowed like mummies
Slumbering in forgotten crates,

Drawings touched with an odd beauty
As if the illustrator had
Responded gravely to the sad
Mementoes of anatomy –

Mysterious candid studies
10   Of red slobland around the bones.
Like this one: flayed men and skeletons
Digging the earth like navvies.

ii

Sad gang of apparitions,
Your skinned muscles like plaited sedge
And your spines hooped towards the sunk edge
Of the spade, my patient ones,

Tell me, as you labour hard
To break this unrelenting soil,
What barns are there for you to fill?
20   What farmer dragged you from the boneyard?

Or are you emblems of the truth,
Death's lifers, hauled from the narrow cell
And stripped of night-shirt shrouds, to tell:
'This is the reward of faith

In rest eternal. Even death
Lies. The void deceives.
We do not fall like autumn leaves
To sleep in peace. Some traitor breath

Revives our clay, sends us abroad
30   And by the sweat of our stripped brows
We earn our deaths; our one repose
When the bleeding instep finds its spade.'

(1975)

TOM SCOTT (1918–   )

Scott began by writing poetry in English but, dissatisfied with the results, took to Scots in the 1940s. His first published collection, *Seeven Poems o Maister Francis Villon* (1953), finds an extremely apt idiom for Villon through the medium of medieval Scots.

It is not such a great distance from Villon to 'Le Crépuscule du Soir', a panorama of the ills and weary perseverance of urban society, and Scott's angular idiolect seems quite at home here.

Gloamin   XCV
frae Baudelaire

Comes the gloamin hour, the cut-throat's freend;
Comes on sleekit fuit wi wowfish mien.
The lift[1] like an auditorium dims doun,
And man waits till his change to beast comes roun.

O Nicht! O freendly nicht, fair dear ti men
Whase airms and harns can say: 'This day, Guid kens,
We've duin our darg!'[2] The nicht alane can cure
The faroush pain in eident spreits and dour –
The trauchlit[3] scholar's, as he rubs his brou;
10   The forfairn[4] workman's, hapt in the bedclaes nou.

Bylins the air's malorous deils again
Sweirtlie[5] steir theirsels like businessmen
To jow[6] in their flicht the gable-ends and shutters.
Frae thir red lamps the wind shaks owre the gutters,
Like some ant-hill that opens wide its doors,

1. *lift*: sky   2. *darg*: task   3. *trauchlit*: harassed   4. *forfairn*: tired-out
5. *sweirtlie*: unwillingly   6. *jow*: shake

Streets are lichtit by the sauls o whures.
Like traitors aye some dernlike[7] wey they shaw
Ti chiels that kill guid-livin at a blaw.
They steir[8] the glaur[9] o ilka toun's main street
20   Like scoyan[10] worms fowk dinna ken they eat.

Here and there ye smell a kitchen's brew,
Hear theatres roar, some band channer[11] and mew.
Mirklan cafes, spivs' haunts and their ilk,
Fill up wi pimps and whures in crepe and silk,
And picklocks, saikless o guid sense or thocht
Cantilie[12] gang ti the yae darg they're aucht,
Cannilie forsin windae, safe and lock
For daily breid – and cled some doxie's dock.[13]

Steel yoursel in this mirk nicht, my saul!
30   Turn a deif ear tae yon caiterwaul.
This is the hour when seikly fowk get waur.
The mirk nicht grips them by the throat, and owre
They gang, inti the pit whaur they began.
The wards are fu o their sichin – mair nor ane
Winnae come back to preive[14] the Sunday jynt
By the fire, nor clek wi cronies owre a pint.

Ay, maist o them hae never kent a hame,
Nor muckle else in life forbye their name.

(1963)

---

7. *dernlike*: secret   8. *steir*: stir up   9. *glaur*: mud
10. *scoyan*: twisting   11. *channer*: complain   12. *cantilie*: happily
13. *dock*: arse   14. *preive*: taste

'Je n'ai pas oublié . . .'

This short, apparently simple poem with its purely allusive treatment of the poet's childhood forms a striking contrast with the verbose and histrionic 'Bénédiction' which opens 'Spleen et Idéal'. When Laforgue described Baudelaire as writing short poems '*sans sujet appréciable*' which left the mystified bourgeois asking '*Et après?*' ('Then what?' or 'So what?'), this is probably the kind of poem he had in mind. It has elicited some effective and moving translations.

XCIX

Je n'ai pas oublié, voisine de la ville,
Notre blanche maison, petite mais tranquille;
Sa Pomone de plâtre et sa vieille Vénus
Dans un bosquet chétif cachant leurs membres nus,
Et le soleil, le soir, ruisselant et superbe,
Qui, derrière la vitre où se brisait sa gerbe,
Semblait, grand œil ouvert dans le ciel curieux,
Contempler nos dîners longs et silencieux,
Répandant largement ses beaux reflets de cierge
10   Sur la nappe frugale et les rideaux de serge.

EDNA ST VINCENT MILLAY

A Memory   XCIX

All this was long ago, but I do not forget
Our small white house, between the city and the farms;
The Venus, the Pomona, – I remember yet

How in the leaves they hid their chipping plaster charms;
And the majestic sun at evening, setting late,
Behind the pane that broke and scattered his bright rays,
How like an open eye he seemed to contemplate
Our long and silent dinners with a curious gaze:
The while his golden beams, like tapers burning there,
10   Made splendid the serge curtains and the simple fare.

(1936)

VERNON WATKINS

I Have Not Forgotten   XCIX

I have not forgotten, neighbouring the town,
Our white house, diminutive, yet where peace brims,
Its plaster Pomona and its Venus age-worn
In a mean, wasted shrubbery hiding their naked limbs,
And at evening the sun, pouring light in disdain,
Which, behind the rich window that broke up its grain,
Seemed, great prying eye in the sky's curious urn,
To watch our slow dinners, prolonged and taciturn,
Displaying its fair, waxen rays to the verge
10   Of the set, frugal cloth and the curtains of serge.

(1956)

ANTHONY HECHT

'Je n'ai pas oublié, voisine de la ville . . .'   XCIX

I remember it well enough, on the edge of town,
That little house, and its quiet, and out in back
The fertile goddesses, naked Venus and so on,
Up to their plaster breasts in wild sumac;
And the sun at evening, flooding the whole place,
Ignited the window with bursting Catherine wheels,
And seemed like a great eye in a prying face,
Watching our mute, interminable meals
And diffusing its votive radiance on all shapes,
10   On the frowsy tablecloth, the worsted drapes.

(1961)

RICHARD HOWARD

I Have Not Forgotten . . .   XCIX

I have not forgotten the house we lived in then,
it was just outside of town, a little white house
in a skimpy grove that hid the naked limbs
of plaster goddesses – the Venus was chipped!
Nor those seemingly endless evenings when the sun
(whose rays ignited every windowpane)
seemed, like a wide eye in the wondering sky,

to contemplate our long silent meals,
kindling more richly than any candlelight
10   the cheap curtains and the much-laundered cloth.

(1982)

La servante au grand cœur . . .

Like the preceding poem, this one seems to have its roots in childhood
relationships. Its language is similarly simple, though the images are not
so cryptic. Peculiar to this poem are the echoes of the nurse's own
speech: 'Nous devrions pourtant . . .' ('We really ought to . . .'); 'Les
pauvres morts ont de grandes douleurs.' This homeliness is particularly well
captured in Lerner's version.

C

La servante au grand cœur dont vous étiez jalouse,
Et qui dort son sommeil sous une humble pelouse,
Nous devrions pourtant lui porter quelques fleurs.
Les morts, les pauvres morts, ont de grandes douleurs,
Et quand Octobre souffle, émondeur des vieux arbres,
Son vent mélancolique à l'entour de leurs marbres,
Certe, ils doivent trouver les vivants bien ingrats,
A dormir, comme ils font, chaudement dans leurs draps,
Tandis que, dévorés de noires songeries,
10   Sans compagnon de lit, sans bonnes causeries,
Vieux squelettes gelés travaillés par le ver,
Ils sentent s'égoutter les neiges de l'hiver
Et le siècle couler, sans qu'amis ni famille
Remplacent les lambeaux qui pendent à leur grille.

Lorsque la bûche siffle et chante, si le soir,
Calme, dans le fauteuil je la voyais s'asseoir,
Si, par une nuit bleue et froide de décembre,
Je la trouvais tapie en un coin de ma chambre,
Grave, et venant du fond de son lit éternel
20 *Couver l'enfant grandi de son œil maternel,*
Que pourrais-je répondre à cette âme pieuse,
Voyant tomber des pleurs de sa paupière creuse?

ROBERT LOWELL

The Servant   C

My old nurse and servant, whose great heart
made you jealous, is dead and sleeps apart
from us. Shouldn't we bring her a few flowers?
The dead, the poor dead, they have their bad hours,
and when October, stripper of old trees,
poisons the turf and makes their marble freeze,
surely they find us worse than wolves or curs
for sleeping under mountainous warm furs . . .
These, eaten by the earth's black dream, lie dead,
10   without a wife or friend to warm their bed,
old skeletons sunk like shrubs in burlap bags –
and feel the ages trickle through their rags.
They have no heirs or relatives to chase
with children round their crosses and replace
the potted refuse, where they lie beneath
their final flower, the interment wreath.

The oak log sings and sputters in my chamber,
and in the cold blue half-light of December,

I see her tiptoe through my room, and halt
20   humbly, as if she'd hurried from her vault
with blankets for the child her sleepless eye
had coaxed and mothered to maturity.
What can I say to her to calm her fears?
My nurse's hollow sockets fill with tears.

(1961)

LAURENCE LERNER

The Nurse   C

You can forget your jealousy: my nurse,
Asleep at last, lies underneath the grass.
We ought at least to take her a few flowers:
For when October shakes down leaves in showers
Around her headstone, and the battered trees
Fill the quiet graveyard with their elegies,
What must she think of us, asleep in bed?
You wouldn't like it either, being dead.
Warm in our sheets we whisper all night long:
10   Eaten by nightmares, silent, shivering.
Inhabited by worms, they lie alone
And listen to the snow upon the stone,
And listen as the years flow by above.
No friend or lover comes to mend their grave.

And if one night, December wild outside,
I found her sitting gravely at my side,
If while the fire sang to the frosty air
I turned towards the wall, and she was there,
Unnoticed in my armchair, shrinking, bent,

20   Come back to brood, a timid revenant,
        With her maternal eye upon her child
        No more a child, alas – what should I find
        To answer her, my dead and pious dear,
        Seeing those hollow eyeballs ooze a tear.

                                              (1967)

ROBERT SYKES (1966–   )

Robert Sykes is one of the editors of this volume.

Mist and Rain   CI

        Fag-end of autumn, winter, mud-drenched spring,
        seasons of sloth, it's you I love and sing
        who swaddle up my heart and my poor brain
        in a tomb of air, a shroud of misty rain.

        In this great flood-plain where the storm-winds sound,
        where all night long the weathercock whirls round,
        my soul – which cowered when buds were opening –
        arches the panoply of its black rook's wing.

        O pallid seasons, Empresses of weather!
10   nothing's more welcome to a morbid heart
        splayed raw beneath the frost's incessant dart

        than your wan shadows which seem set for ever.
        – Save one night, while the moon averts her face,
        to rock my grief to sleep in a chance embrace . . .

                                              (1997)

EDNA ST VINCENT MILLAY

'Rêve Parisien' was dedicated to Constantin Guys, the painter whom
Baudelaire celebrates in his essay 'Le Peintre de la Vie Moderne'.

Parisian Dream   CII

i

That marvellous landscape of my dream –
Which no eye knows, nor ever will –
At moments, wide awake, I seem
To grasp, and it excites me still.

Sleep, how miraculous you are –
A strange caprice had urged my hand
To banish, as irregular,
All vegetation from that land;

And, proud of what my art had done,
10   I viewed my painting, knew the great
Intoxicating monotone
Of marble, water, steel and slate.

Staircases and arcades there were
In a long labyrinth, which led
To a vast palace; fountains there
Were gushing gold, and gushing lead.

And many a heavy cataract
Hung like a curtain, – did not fall,
As water does, but hung, compact,
20   Crystal, on many a metal wall.

Tall nymphs with Titan breasts and knees
Gazed at their images unblurred,
Where groves of colonnades, not trees,
Fringed a deep pool where nothing stirred.

Blue sheets of water, left and right,
Spread between quays of rose and green,
To the world's end and out of sight,
And still expanded, though unseen.

Enchanted rivers, those – with jade
30   And jasper were their banks bedecked;
Enormous mirrors, dazzled, made
Dizzy by all they did reflect.

And many a Ganges, taciturn
And heedless, in the vaulted air,
Poured out the treasure of its urn
Into a gulf of diamond there.

As architect, it tempted me
To tame the ocean at its source;
And this I did, – I made the sea
40   Under a jeweled culvert course.

And every colour, even black,
Became prismatic, polished, bright;
The liquid gave its glory back
Mounted in iridescent light.

There was no moon, there was no sun, –
For why should sun and moon conspire
To light such prodigies? – each one
Blazed with its own essential fire!

A silence like eternity
50   Prevailed, there was no sound to hear;
These marvels all were for the eye,
And there was nothing for the ear.

ii

I woke; my mind was bright with flame;
I saw the cheap and sordid hole
I live in, and my cares all came
Burrowing back into my soul.

Brutally the twelve strokes of noon
Against my naked ear were hurled
And a grey sky was drizzling down
60   Upon this sad, lethargic world.

(1936)

Dawn   CIII

Outside the barracks now the bugle called, and woke
The morning wind, which rose, making the lanterns smoke.

It was that hour when tortured dreams of stealthy joys
Twist in their beds the thin brown bodies of growing boys;
When, like a blood-shot eye that blinks and looks away,
The lamp still burns, and casts a red stain on the day;
When the soul, pinned beneath the body's weight and brawn,
Strives, as the lamplight strives to overcome the dawn;
The air, like a sad face whose tears the breezes dry,
10   Is tremulous with countless things about to die;
And men grow tired of writing, and women of making love.

Blue smoke was curling now from the cold chimneys of
A house or two; with heavy lids, mouths open wide,
Prostitutes slept their slumber dull and stupefied;
While labourers' wives got up, with sucked-out breasts, and
    stood
Blowing first on their hands, then on the flickering wood.
It was that hour when cold, and lack of things they need,
Combine, and women in childbirth have it hard indeed.
Like a sob choked by frothy hemorrhage, somewhere
20   Far-off a sudden cock-crow tore the misty air;
A sea of fog rolled in, effacing roofs and walls;
The dying, that all night in the bare hospitals
Had fought for life, grew weaker, rattled, and fell dead;
And gentlemen, debauched and drunk, swayed home to bed.

Aurora now in a thin dress of green and rose,
With chattering teeth advanced. Old sombre Paris rose,
Picked up its tools, and, over the deserted Seine,
Yawning, rubbing its eyes, slouched forth to work again.

(1936)

ANTHONY RYLE

A very precise rendering of meaning. The choice of free verse is
surprising, however, given that the original makes very deliberate use
of traditional rhyming couplets.

Daybreak   CIII

The reveille sounds in the barracks;
In the streets
Lamps flicker in the first breeze.

It is the hour when evil dreams
Agitate adolescent beds,
When the lamp,
A throbbing, evil eye,
Stains the day red;
When the soul's resistance
10   To the crude, heavy body
Imitates this battle
Of lamp and day.
Like a weeping face
Dried by the wind
The air shivers
With things in flight;
Desire ebbs
From the man writing,
The woman loving.

20   Smoke curls
From the first chimneys;
Stupified mascara'd whores
Gape open-mouthed;
Scraggy-breasted beggarwormen
Blow on their cold fingers,
Blow on hot coals.
At this hour,
Amidst the cold and shame,
Labour pains strike more sharply;
30   Cockcrow cuts the mist
Like a sob
Choked on bloody froth.
Fog laps the buildings.
In the depths of hospitals
Come the irregular gasps
And last rattle of the dying.
Exhausted by debauchery
Rakes return home.

Shivering dawn
40   In her pink and green
Creeps along the deserted Seine;
Rubbing his eyes
The sombre and hardworking
Old Man Paris
Picks up his tools.

(1995)

LAURENCE LERNER

Morning Twilight   CIII

Morning. The bugle sounds. The streetlamps shake
In the dawn wind. Slowly the houses wake.

A swarm of nightmares twisting their dark heads,
The adolescents disarrange their beds.
Throbbing and turning like a Cyclop's eye,
My lamp is a red stain upon the day.
The soul beneath its weight of blood and bone
Enacts that conflict of the lamp and dawn.
The air is damp, with tears upon its skin,
10   It trembles; the breeze dries its face.
                                        A man
Throws down his pen; the woman turns her back,
Saying, 'Enough.' The chimneys start to smoke.
Stupid with sex, the whores upon their beds
Drop off to sleep with aching heads.
A beggar woman pokes the dying brands,
Rubs her thin breasts, and blows upon her hands.

Women in labour close their eyes in pain;
Their screams redouble as the day is born.
20 Like a consumptive sobbing in his chest
A cock crows somewhere, tearing at the mist.

The roofs are islands in a ghostly sea.
This is death's moment. Unremittingly
He walks the wards for victims, and they choke.
Young men in evening dress stroll through the park
Or step from taxis, tired with the night's work.

Dawn shivers as it slinks across the Seine,
Wearing its dressing-gown of pink and green,
And Paris, poor old horse, blinks its tired eyes,
30 Feeling the harness tighten on its flesh.

(1967)

Le Vin

Wine

GEORGE DILLON

Baudelaire's notebooks show that he was at one time thinking of writing a play on the same macabre theme as that of this poem. The language of the original is, for the most part, unusually familiar: it is written as a kind of dramatic monologue for a working man. At other times, however, notably in stanza ten, it breathes a tired, 'black' romanticism that sits very ill with the supposed character of the speaker. Dillon manages the colloquialism pretty well; the uneasiness of tone in his version mirrors that of the original.

The Drunkard   CVI

My wife is dead, and I am free!
Now I can drink both night and day.
When I came home without my pay
Her crying upset me horribly.

I am as happy as a king.
The air is soft. The sky is clear.
Ah, what a lovely spring, this year!
I courted her in such a spring.

Now I can drink to drown my care
10   As much wine as her tomb would hold –
The tomb where she lies pale and cold.
And that will be no small affair,

For I have thrown her, body and limb,
In an old well; I even threw
All the loose stones around the brim
On top of her. Good riddance, too!

I asked her in the name of Christ,
To whom our marriage vows were told,
To be my sweetheart as of old –
20   To come to a forsaken tryst

We had when we were young and gay,
That everything might be the same;
And she, the foolish creature, came!
We all have our weak moments, eh?

She was attractive still, all right,
Though faded. I still loved her – more
Than there was rhyme or reason for.
I had to end it, come what might!

Nobody understands me. What's
30   The use of wasting my good breath
Explaining to these stupid sots
The mysteries of love and death?

They take their women by routine,
These louts – the way they eat and drink.
Which one has ever stopped to think
What the word love might really mean?

Love, with its softness in your reins,
With all its nightmares, all its fears,
Its cups of poison mixed with tears,
40   Its rattling skeletons and chains.

– Well, here I am, alone and free!
Tonight I will be drunk for fair,
And I will lay me down, I swear,
Upon the highroad happily,

And sleep like an old dog, be sure,
Right where the heavy trucks go by,
Loaded with gravel and manure.
The wheel can smear my brains out – ay,

Or it can break me like a clod
50 In two, or it can mash me flat.
I care about as much for that
As for the long white beard of God!

(1936)

F. P. STURM

The Wine of Lovers   CVIII

Space rolls to-day her splendour round!
Unbridled, spurless, without bound,
Mount we upon the wings of wine
For skies fantastic and divine!

Let us, like angels tortured by
Some wild delirious phantasy,
Follow the far-off mirage born
In the blue crystal of the morn.

And gently balanced on the wing
10 Of the wild whirlwind we will ride,
Rejoicing with the joyous thing.

My sister, floating side by side,
Fly we unceasing whither gleams
The distant heaven of my dreams.

(1906)

Fleurs du Mal

Flowers of Evil

VINCENT O'SULLIVAN
(1868–1940)

O'Sullivan left Oxford after one term, in 1892, and began to frequent literary circles. He became a close friend of Ernest Dowson and Aubrey Beardsley, and later of Oscar Wilde, who admired his poetry and whom he supported financially on his release from prison. He produced two collections of verse (from the first of which his solitary Baudelaire translation is taken) in a determinedly Decadent vein. Thereafter he abandoned poetry in favour of fiction and journalism, living most of his life in France and dying impoverished in Paris just before it fell to the Germans.

Destruction   CIX

The Devil stirs about me without rest,
And round me floats like noxious air and thin;
I breathe this poison-air which scalds my breast,
And fills me with desires of monstrous sin.

Knowing my love of Art, he sometimes takes
The shape of supple girls supremely fair;
And with a wily, canting lie he makes
My heated lips his shameful potions share.

Then far he leads me from the sight of God,
Crushed with fatigue, to where no man has trod –
To the vague, barren plains where silence sounds,

And hurls into my face his foul construction
Of slimy clothes, and gaping, putrid wounds,
And all the bleeding harness of Destruction!

                                                                    (1896)

EDNA ST VINCENT MILLAY

Murdered Woman   CX
DRAWING OF AN UNKNOWN MASTER

Flasks of expensive scent, embroideries, rich brocades,
        Taffeta sofas, satin chairs;
Statues in marble, paintings; fragrance that pervades
        The empty, sumptuous gowns; warm airs

And sweet, – yet sultry, damp, unhealthful to inhale:
        That sickening green-house atmosphere
Dying bouquets in their glass coffins give – a stale
        Voluptuous chamber . . . Lying here

A corpse without a head, whence flows in a bright stream,
10   Making an ever broadening stain,
The red and living blood, which the white pillows seem
        To lap up like a thirsty plain.

Pale as those awful shapes that out of shadow stare,
        Chaining our helpless eyes to theirs,
The head, with its great mass of rich and sombre hair –
        The ear-rings still in the small ears –

Like a ranunculus on the night-table sits;
        And, void of thought, blank as the light
Of dawn, a glinting vague regard escapes from its
20   Eyeballs, up-rolled and china-white.

The headless trunk, in shameless posture on the bed,
        Naked, in loose abandon lies,
Its secret parts exposed, its treasures all outspread
        As if to charm a lover's eyes.

One sequined stocking, pink against the milky thigh,
        Remains, pathetic souvenir;
The jeweled garter, like a flashing, secret eye,
        Darts and withdraws a diamond leer.

A languorous portrait on the wall contrives to give
30   Force to the singular effect
Of the deep solitude, – the eyes provocative,
        The pose inviting, half-erect.

The ghost of something strange and guilty, of some feast
        Involving most improper fare,
Demoniac kisses, all obscure desires released,
        Swims in the silent curtains there.

And yet, that fragile shoulder, that fine hand and arm –
        How delicate the curve they make! –
The pelvic bones so sweetly pointed, the whole form
40   Lithe as a teased and fighting snake! –

She must have been quite young . . . her senses, all her soul,
        Avid for life and driven wild
By tedium, set ajar, it may be, to the whole
        Pack of perversions . . . ah, poor child!

Did he at length, that man, his awful thirst too great
        For living flesh to satisfy,
On this inert, obedient body consummate
        His lust? – O ravished corpse, reply!

Answer me, impure thing! Speak, frightening head, and tell:
50   Lifting you up by your long hair,
Did he on your cold teeth imprint in last farewell
        One kiss, before he set you there?

Far from the mocking world, the peering crowd, oh far
    From inquest, coroner, magistrate,
Sleep; sleep in peace; I leave you lying as you are,
    Mysterious unfortunate.

In vain your lover roves the world; the thought of you
    Troubles each chamber where he lies:
Even as you are true to him, he will be true
60   To you, no doubt, until he dies.

(1936)

SIR ERIC MACLAGAN (1879–1951)

Director of the Victoria and Albert Museum from 1924 to 1945, Sir
Eric Maclagan was a man of deep learning and wide artistic interests.
He published a volume of verse while an undergraduate at Christ
Church, Oxford; thereafter poetry appears to have been an occasional
pursuit. The metrical poise and finely judged rhetoric of his translation
of 'Femmes Damnées' (one of three published for the first time by
James Laver in his anthology) more than compensate for occasional
quaintnesses of diction and announce a genuine poet who is also an
accurate and sensitive translator. Maclagan also produced versions of
Rimbaud and Valéry.

Women Accurst   CXI

Like brooding cattle crouched along the sands
To the sea's utmost verge they turn their eyes,
And their feet mingle, and their groping hands
Learn bitter shudderings, languid ecstasies.

Some, whom unending confidences please,
Spell out their tales of timid girlish love,
And score the green bark of the sapling trees
Where the brook babbles through the hidden grove;

Others, a solemn sisterhood they seem,
Through spectre-haunted crags are moving slow,
Where naked breasts rose like a lava stream
And flushed for tempted Anthony long ago.

These, where the flaring torches drip with gum
In some old pagan cavern, hushed and deep,
Bid Bacchus heal their fevered moans, and come
To lull the memories of remorse to sleep.

And these, whose bosoms crave the scapular,
Who hide a scourge beneath the gowns they train,
Mix in lone nights, in shadowy woods afar,
The froth of pleasure with the tears of pain.

Ah virgins, demons, monsters, martyr host,
High souls, that dare reality despise,
Saints, satyrs, pilgrims for the infinite coast,
Now prodigal of tears, and now of cries,

Poor sisters, all my pity and love are yours
Whom to that hell my spirit has pursued,
For the dull pain, the thirst that still endures,
The tide of passion in your hearts renewed.

(1940)

ARTHUR SYMONS

An inventive version to say the least! 'Two detestable Hags' translates '*deux aimables filles*'. (Literal translation by CC.)

The Two Good Sisters CXII

Debauch and Death are two detestable Hags,
Rich and ribald and of kisses prodigal,
Whose virginal wombs are always draped in rags,
Whose fervent ardours are demi-virginal.*

To the Sinister Poet, enemy of men's money-bags,
Favourite of Hell, Courtesan and Cardinal,
Tombs and brothels show under the infernal flags
A bed remorse frequented never, maniacal.†

And the coffin and the alcove pregnant to bestir me
10 Offer to all of us, like two sisters, listless leisures,
Fearful sweetnesses and intolerable pleasures.‡

* Debauchery and Death are two good-hearted girls, free with their kisses and rich in good health, whose loins, ever virgin and draped in rags, though eternally ploughed, have never borne fruit.
† To the sinister poet, enemy of families, favourite of hell, ill-provided courtier, tombs and brothels offer, under their arbours, a bed where remorse has never laid its head.
‡ And the bier and the alcove abounding in blasphemies offer us in turn, like two kind sisters, terrible pleasures and hideous sweetnesses.

Debauch, with unclean arms, when will you enter me?
O Death, when will you, her rival, her wiles being quaffed,
On her black cypresses your infected myrtles ingraft?*

(1925)

Un Voyage à Cythère

Cythera is the legendary island of love, and the embarkation for Cythera, depicted by eighteenth-century *fête galante* painters, notably Watteau, symbolized the beginning of a sexual liaison. Stanzas three, four and six with their repeated evocations of beauty, their myrtle shades, scented breezes, roses, doves and provokingly semi-nude priestess, recall Boucher's erotic treatment of mythological subjects, and repeatedly postpone our confrontation with bleak, present-day reality. The latter part of the poem delights in horror, but horror relieved by irony: there is a strange combination of self-dramatization and self-mockery ('*Ridicule pendu . . . pauvre diable . . .*').

A later poet would not have allowed himself the '*gibet symbolique*' of the last stanza, and we note how all our translators avoid it. ('Token' is very far from the sense of the original.)

* When will you bury me, o Debauchery of the unclean arms? O Death, her rival in attraction, when will you come and, upon her stinking myrtle, graft your black cypress boughs?

Un Voyage à Cythère   CXVI

Mon cœur, comme un oiseau, voltigeait tout joyeux
Et planait librement à l'entour des cordages;
Le navire roulait sous un ciel sans nuages,
Comme un ange enivré d'un soleil radieux.

Quelle est cette île triste et noire? — C'est Cythère,
Nous dit-on, un pays fameux dans les chansons,
Eldorado banal de tous les vieux garçons.
Regardez, après tout, c'est une pauvre terre.

— Ile des doux secrets et des fêtes du cœur!
10   De l'antique Vénus le superbe fantôme
Au-dessus de tes mers plane comme un arôme,
Et charge les esprits d'amour et de langueur.

Belle île aux myrtes verts, pleine de fleurs écloses,
Vénérée à jamais par toute nation,
Où les soupirs des cœurs en adoration
Roulent comme l'encens sur un jardin de roses

Ou le roucoulement éternal d'un ramier!
— Cythère n'était plus qu'un terrain des plus maigres,
Un désert rocailleux troublé par des cris aigres.
20   J'entrevoyais pourtant un objet singulier!

Ce n'était pas un temple aux ombres bocagères,
Où la jeune prêtresse, amoureuse des fleurs,
Allait, le corps brûlé de secrètes chaleurs,
Entrebâillant sa robe aux brises passagères;

Mais voilà qu'en rasant la côte d'assez près
Pour troubler les oiseaux avec nos voiles blanches,
Nous vîmes que c'était un gibet à trois branches,
Du ciel se détachant en noir, comme un cyprès.

De féroces oiseaux perchés sur leur pâture
30 *Détruisaient avec rage un pendu déjà mûr,*
Chacun plantant, comme un outil, son bec impur
Dans tous les coins saignants de cette pourriture;

Les yeux étaient deux trous, et du ventre effondré
Les intestins pesants lui coulaient sur les cuisses,
Et ses bourreaux, gorgés de hideuses délices,
L'avaient à coups de bec absolument châtré.

Sous les pieds, un troupeau de jaloux quadrupèdes,
Le museau relevé, tournoyait et rôdait;
Une plus grande bête au milieu s'agitait
40 *Comme un exécuteur entouré de ses aides.*

Habitant de Cythère, enfant d'un ciel si beau,
Silencieusement tu souffrais ces insultes
En expiation de tes infâmes cultes
Et des péchés qui t'ont interdit le tombeau.

Ridicule pendu, tes douleurs sont les miennes!
Je sentis, à l'aspect de tes membres flottants,
Comme un vomissement, remonter vers mes dents
Le long fleuve de fiel des douleurs anciennes;

Devant toi, pauvre diable au souvenir si cher,
50 *J'ai senti tous les becs et toutes les mâchoires*
Des corbeaux lancinants et des panthères noires
Qui jadis aimaient tant à triturer ma chair.

– Le ciel était charmant, la mer était unie;
Pour moi tout était noir et sanglant désormais,
Hélas! et j'avais, comme en un suaire épais,
Le cœur enseveli dans cette allégorie.

Dans ton île, ô Vénus! je n'ai trouvé debout
Qu'un gibet symbolique où pendait mon image . . .
– Ah! Seigneur! donnez-moi la force et le courage
60 *De contempler mon cœur et mon corps sans dégoût!*

ROY CAMPBELL

Voyage to Cytherea   CXVI

My heart, a bird, seemed joyfully to fly
And round the rigging cruised with nimble gyre.
The vessel rolled beneath the cloudless sky
Like a white angel, drunk with solar fire.

What is that sad, black island like a pall?
Why, Cytherea, famed in many a book,
The Eldorado of old-stagers. Look:
It's but a damned poor country after all!

Isle of sweet secrets and heart-feasting fire!
10 Of antique Venus the majestic ghost
Rolls like a storm of fragrance from your coast
Filling our souls with languor and desire!

Isle of green myrtles, where each flower uncloses,
Adored by nations till the end of time:
Sighs of adoring hearts, like incense, climb.
And pour their perfume over sheaves of roses,

Or groves of turtles in an endless coo!
But no! it was a waste where nothing grows,
Torn only by the raucous cries of crows:
20   Yet there a curious object rose in view.

This was no temple hid in bosky trees,
Where the young priestess, amorous of flowers,
Whom secretly a loving flame devours,
Walks with her robe half-open to the breeze.

For as we moved inshore to coast the shallows
And our white canvas scared the crows to fly,
Like a tall cypress, blackened on the sky,
We saw it was a gaunt three-forking gallows.

Fierce birds, perched on their meal, began to slash
30   And rip with rage a rotten corpse that swung.
Each screwed and chiselled with its beak among
The crisp and bleeding crannies of the hash.

His eyes were holes: from open stomach direly
His heavy tripes cascaded to his thighs.
Gorged with such ghastly dainties to the eyes,
His torturers had gelded him entirely.

Beneath, some jealous prowling quadrupeds,
With lifted muzzles, for the leavings scrambled.
The largest seemed, as in the midst he gambolled,
40   An executioner among his *aides*.

Native of Cytherea's cloudless clime
In silent suffering you paid the price,
And expiated ancient cults of vice
With generations of forbidden crime.

Ridiculous hanged man! Your griefs I know.
I felt, to see you swing above the heath,
Like nausea slowly rising to my teeth,
The bilious stream of ancient human woe.

Poor devil, dear to memory! before me
50   I seemed to feel each talon, fang, and beak
Of all the stinking crows and panthers sleek
That in my lifetime ever chewed and tore me.

The sky was charming and the sea unclouded,
But all was black and bloody to my mind.
As in a dismal winding-sheet entwined,
My heart was in this allegory shrouded.

A gallows where my image hung apart
Was all I found on Venus' isle of sighs.
O God, give me the strength to scrutinise,
60   Without disgust, my body and my heart!

(1952)

RICHARD HOWARD

A Voyage to Cythera   CXVI

My heart flew up like a bird before the mast,
circled the shrouds and mounted free and clear;
the ship rolled on beneath a cloudless sky
like an angel drunk on the glory of the sun.

What is that dreary island – the black one there?
Cythera, someone says, the one in the song
insipid Eldorado of good old boys:
it isn't much of a place, as you can see.

Island of feasting hearts and secret joys!
10   Like a fragrance, the voluptuary ghost
of Aphrodite floats above your shores,
inflaming minds with languor and with love.

Island green with myrtle, rich with bloom,
revered forever by all mortal men
from whose adoring hearts wells up a sigh
soft as the fallen petals of a rose

or the relentless moan of doves . . . Cythera now
was nothing more than a thistled promontory
vexed by the wheeling gulls' unruly cries.
20   Yet there was something . . . I could see it now;

no temple sheltered by its sacred grove,
no priestess gathering blossoms, her loose robe
half-opened to the breezes as they passed,
her flesh ignited by a secret fire;

but as we cleared the coastline – close enough
to scare the shorebirds with our flapping sails –
we saw what it was: black against the sky,
no cypress but a branching gallows-tree.

Perched on their provender, ferocious birds
30   were ravaging the ripe corpse hanging there,
driving their filthy beaks like cruel drills
into each cranny of its rotten flesh;

the eyes were holes, and from the ruined groin
a coil of heavy guts had tumbled out –
the greedy creatures, gorged on hideous sweets,
had peck by vicious peck castrated him.

Below his feet, among a whining pack
that waited, muzzles lifted for their share,
some bigger beast was prowling back and forth
40   like a hangman huge among his underlings.

Inhabitant of Cythera, rapture's child,
how silently you suffered these affronts
in expiation of your shameful rites
and sins that have proscribed your burial.

Ludicrous carcass! I hung there with you,
and at the sight of your insulted limbs
I tasted, like a vomit in my mouth,
the bitter tide of age-old sufferings.

Knowing what you were and what you are,
50   I felt each saber-tooth and jabbing beak
of jet-black panthers and of carrion-crows
that once so loved to lacerate my flesh.

. . . The sky was suave, the sea serene; for me
from now on everything was bloody and black
– the worse for me – and as if in a shroud
my heart lay buried in this allegory.

On Aphrodite's island all I found
was a token gallows where my image hung . . .
Lord give me strength and courage to behold
60   my body and my heart without disgust!

(1982)

BASIL BUNTING (1900–1985)

An Englishman, Bunting was formed as a writer in the inter-war expatriate milieu, working in Paris on Ford Madox Ford's *Transatlantic Review*, and moving to Italy in the wake of Ezra Pound, who was a major influence on his complex, allusive, cross-cultural poetry. His craggy modernism won him a reputation in America, but he did not come to prominence in Britain until the publication of *Briggflatts* (1966), a long, searching meditation on his Northumbrian roots. He produced numerous translations of poetry, especially from Persian and Latin, which he termed his 'Overdrafts', a sobriquet indicative of his imaginative, Poundian attitude to the business of translation.

In *Baudelaire in Cythera* (written in or before 1935, but first published in *Uncollected Poems*, 1991) the main substance of the poem is rendered accurately, though with a brusque compression that drags the original's suggestion of a thwarted idyll into the twentieth century and an English rather than a French milieu. The final two lines are condensed from the original's sixteen, and substitute for the rhetorical addresses to the corpse and to God an allusion to the poet's real-life misfortunes: it was reported that after his last stroke Baudelaire could no longer recognize his reflection in the mirror and bowed to it politely, as if to a stranger.

Baudelaire in Cythera   CXVI
(after Baudelaire)

Heart trapezing gaily about the ropes: hull
a-roll under a clear sky.

                              – That sombre beach?
– Songfamous Cythera.

                              – Indeed?

                                        – Yes,
bachelor's paradise. Look at it . . . wretched place!
Festivals of love, eh? . . . whispers and all that?

The moist smell of amours clings to it, isle of blown
10   roses, still adored. Devout whimpers drift
above like pollen, like ringdove murmurs. A harsh
stony hungry land, harassed by shrill cries.
Nothing Baedeker stars: though I did see something . . .

Not a temple shaded by ancient planes, nor yet
a young priestess of love slacking her tunic to
feel the breeze. We ranged very close in shore,
so close our sails set the birds fluttering over a
black gallows cut out of the sky.

                                 They were perched on
20   carrion, their beaks driven precisely into
putrid sores. The eyes, rotted. Heavy bowels
dangling. Vultures had castrated him. Dogs
were howling.

            Cytherean!
Child of sublime skies! Comic corpse, wretched
contemptible corpse!

Bright sky, shining sea, Venus' land; Baudelaire
bows to Baudelaire through the looking-glass.

                                             (1991)

JACKSON MATHEWS (1907–1980)

Mathews made this version for the anthology of English verse trans-
lations of Baudelaire that he edited with his wife Marthiel in 1955. He
was then a Professor of Comparative Literature at the University of
Washington, Seattle.

Love and the Skull   CXVI
(AN OLD CUL-DE-LAMPE)

Love sits astride the very skull
    Of Humanity,
And thus enthroned, the impious fool
    In his effrontery

Laughs and blows bubbles. They gaily swirl
    Upward as if to fly
Away toward some other world
    In the depths of the sky.

Each luminous and fragile whole
10   Soars up, a golden thought,
Then spits its little spray of soul
    Out and is naught.

The skull, at every frail report,
    Groans to the fiend:
'When will this meaningless brutal sport
    Come to an end?

What with your cruel mouth you scatter
  In the air like rain,
Murderous monster, is the matter
20   Of my blood and my brain!'

(1955)

Révolte

Revolt

RICHARD HOWARD

Saint Peter's Denial   CXVIII

The tide of curses day by day ascends
unto His hosts – and God, what does He do?
Like a tyrant gorged on meat and wine, He sleeps –
the sound of our blasphemies sweet in His Ears.

The martyrs' sobs, the screaming at the stake
compose, no doubt, a heady symphony;
indeed, for all the blood their pleasure costs,
the Heavens have not yet had half enough!

Remember the Mount of Olives, Jesus? When
you fell on your knees and humbly prayed to Him
Who laughed on high at the sound of hammering
as the butchers drove the nails into your flesh?

And when they spat on your divinity,
the jeering scullions and the conscript scum –
that moment when you felt the thorns impale
the skull which housed Humanity itself;

when the intolerable weight of your tormented flesh
hung from your distended arms; when blood
and sweat cascaded from your whitening brow;
when you were made a target for all eyes –

did you dream then of the wonder-working days
when you came to keep eternal promises,
riding an ass, and everywhere the ways
strewn with palms and flowers – those were the days!

when, your heart on fire with valor and with hope,
you whipped the moneylenders out of that place –
you were master then! But now, has not remorse
pierced your side even deeper than the spear?

Myself, I shall be satisfied to quit
30   a world where action is no kin to dreams;
would I had used – and perished by – the sword!
Peter denied his Master . . . He did well!

(1982)

JAMES ELROY FLECKER

Litany to Satan   CXIX

O grandest of the Angels, and most wise,
O fallen God, fate-driven from the skies,
Satan, at last take pity on our pain.

O first of exiles who endurest wrong,
Yet growest, in thy hatred, still more strong,
Satan, at last take pity on our pain!

O subterranean King, omniscient,
Healer of man's immortal discontent,
Satan, at last take pity on our pain.

10   To lepers and to outcasts thou dost show
That Passion is the Paradise below.
Satan, at last take pity on our pain.

Thou, by thy mistress Death, hast given to man
Hope, the imperishable courtesan.
Satan, at last take pity on our pain.

Thou givest to the Guilty their calm mien
Which damns the crowd around the guillotine.
Satan, at last take pity on our pain.

Thou knowest the corners of the jealous Earth
20 Where God has hidden jewels of great worth.
Satan, at last take pity on our pain.

Thou stretchest forth a saving hand to keep
Such men as roam upon the roofs in sleep.
Satan, at last take pity on our pain.

Thy power can make the halting Drunkard's feet
Avoid the peril of the surging street.
Satan, at last take pity on our pain.

Thou, to console our helplessness, didst plot
The cunning use of powder and of shot.
30 Satan, at last take pity on our pain.

Thy awful name is written as with pitch
On the unrelenting foreheads of the rich.
Satan, at last take pity on our pain.

In strange and hidden places thou dost move
Where women cry for torture in their love.
Satan, at last take pity on our pain.

Father of those whom God's tempestuous ire
Has flung from Paradise with sword and fire,
Satan, at last take pity on our pain.

PRAYER

40   Satan, to thee be praise upon the Height
         Where thou wast king of old, and in the night
         Of Hell, where thou dost dream on silently.
         Grant that one day beneath the Knowledge-tree,
         When it shoots forth to grace thy royal brow,
         My soul may sit, that cries upon thee now.

                                                    (1907)

La Mort

Death

La Mort des amants *and*
La Mort des pauvres

These two sonnets, very different in style, tempted many of the early translators of Baudelaire, and later elicited strongly contrasting versions from poets of the twentieth century.

La Mort des amants   CXXI

Nous aurons des lits pleins d'odeurs légères,
Des divans – profonds comme des tombeaux,
Et d'étranges fleurs sur des étagères,
Ecloses pour nous sous des cieux plus beaux.

Usant à l'envi leurs chaleurs dernières,
Nos deux cœurs seront deux vastes flambeaux,
Qui réfléchiront leurs doubles lumières
Dans nos deux esprits, ces miroirs jumeaux.

Un soir fait de rose et de bleu mystique,
10   Nous échangerons un éclair unique,
Comme un long sanglot, tout chargé d'adieux;

Et plus tard un Ange, entr'ouvrant les portes,
Viendra ranimer, fidèle et joyeux,
Les miroirs ternis et les flammes mortes.

La Mort des pauvres   CXXII

C'est la Mort qui console, hélas! et qui fait vivre;
C'est le but de la vie, et c'est le seul espoir
Qui, comme un élixir, nous monte et nous enivre,
Et nous donne le cœur de marcher jusqu'au soir;

A travers la tempête, et la neige, et le givre,
C'est la clarté vibrante à notre horizon noir;
C'est l'auberge fameuse inscrite sur le livre,
Où l'on pourra manger, et dormir, et s'asseoir;

C'est un Ange qui tient dans ses doigts magnétiques
10   *Le sommeil et le don des rêves extatiques,*
Et qui refait le lit des gens pauvres et nus;

C'est la gloire des dieux, c'est le grenier mystique,
C'est la bourse du pauvre et sa patrie antique,
C'est le portique ouvert sur les Cieux inconnus!

HENRY CURWEN (1845–92)

Curwen worked in publishing in London before emigrating to India (1876) and joining the staff of the *Times of India*, of which he ultimately became chief editor and co-proprietor. Prior to his departure from England he was much concerned with modern poetry: in addition to his *Echoes from French Poets* (1870), a selection of translations from Baudelaire, Lamartine, Musset and others, he translated Baudelaire's *Edgar-Allen Poe, sa vie et ses ouvrages* (1872) and contributed an intelligent study of Poe himself to the *Westminster Magazine*. He was only the second writer to publish English translations of Baudelaire, and his versions (in *Echoes*) display rather more discrimination, understanding and poetic competence than those of his predecessor by a year, R. H. Shepherd. He is fond of hymn-tune metres which seem more appropriate to the second sonnet than to the first.

The Lover's Death   CXXI

We will have voluptuous couches, full of subtle, faint,
        perfume,
We will have soft clasping cushions, deep and silent as the
        tomb;
Strange flowers on the window ledges, shutting out the azure
        skies,
Tingeing all the sunlight's languor with a thousand crimson
        dyes.

Using, slowly, as if grudging, their consuming, final heat,
Our two hearts will meet together, as two mighty flames might
        meet,
And reflect their double splendour, and their double streams of
        light;
In your soul and mine, my darling, as on mirrors burnish'd
        bright.

On an evening, rosy tinted, and with mystic blue half-dark,
Our two hearts will throb together, and exchange their dying
        spark,
Like a long-drawn sighing, sobbing, overladen with 'farewells'.

Later on will come an angel, floating thro' the open door,
Joyful in his task of mercy, mighty with death-conquering
        spells,
To revive the tarnish'd mirrors, and the shatter'd flames once
        more!

                                                (1870)

HENRY D'AVIGDOR
BLUMBERG (1867–1932)

The son of a Hungarian emigré, Blumberg was to spend all his life as a family doctor and the medical officer of a children's sanatorium in Southport, England. This pattern was only varied by his four years' service in the Great War, in which he was decorated and which provided much of the inspiration for his own poetry. His *Prose and Poetry* (1934) was collected by his sister after his death. It combines translations from Baudelaire and Petöfi with original poems by Henry and his brother Gustav.

The Death of Lovers   CXXI

We shall have couches in soft perfumes steeped,
    Deep dark divans, like tombs, whereon to lie,
And languor-laden flowers in vases heaped
    That blossomed for us 'neath a brighter sky.

And fanning their last embers to a blaze,
    Our hearts will be as torches, thine and mine,
Whose striving flames reflect their double rays
    In the twin mirrors of our souls divine.

One evening, in a mist of rose and blue,
A parting beam shall pass between us two,
Charged with farewells and whispers of sweet names;

And then, an angel throwing wide the gate,
Will come and tenderly reanimate
The tarnished mirrors and the sunken flames.

(1934)

JAMES LIDDY (1934–   )

An Irishman educated at University College, Dublin, Liddy is Professor of English at the University of Wisconsin–Milwaukee. He edited *Arena* during the 1960s; he has produced various collections of poetry and his *Collected Poems* appeared in 1994. *Baudelaire's Bar Flowers* (1975) is a modern recasting, largely from a gay perspective, of poems from *Les Fleurs du Mal*.

The Death of Lovers   CXXI

We'll have beds full of delicate scents
Divans deep as graves
And beneath more beautiful skies
Strange flowers on the shelves
Blossoming
For us.

Using up their last heat our hearts
Will be two huge candles
Reflecting their double light
10   In both our minds
Twin
Mirrors.

In the blue hour
Made of roses we'll exchange
A flash of lightening like a long sob
Orgiastic with
Goodbyes

And then a joyous Angel recipro
Cally opening the doors
20   Will wipe the cloudy mirror
And light the dead
Tapers.

(1975)

HENRY CURWEN

The quatrains would go well to *Hymns Ancient and Modern*, no. 184,
'Jerusalem the Golden'.

The Pauper's Death   CXXII

O Death, the great Consoler. 'Tis he who makes us live,
   He is the aim of life, there is no hope beside;
Elixir-like he rises in our poor brains to give
   Strength, and the will to march, until the eventide.

Death, the flashing Beacon, on which we madly look,
   Longingly, thro' the snow, and thro' the icy blast,
Death the famous hostel, we read of in the Book,
   Where we may eat and drink, and seat ourselves at last.

Death the Angel, holding in his mesmeric fingers
10   Sleep, and the gift of dreams, where joy and beauty lingers,
A warm bed for the weary – a cold tomb for the wise;
Death the glory of God – Garner of coin untold,
Home to the homeless wretch – the pauper's purse of gold,
Death the wond'rous portal, unfolding wond'rous skies!

(1870)

LAURENCE LERNER

The Poor Praise Death   CXXII

Death's all we have, to comfort or to goad,
To mount our hopes, to give us heart to trudge
Uphill till evening on the endless road,
Wet through with rain and stumbling in the sludge:

Death is our deepest wish, our one delight,
The patch of sunlight in the stormy west.
There has to be a shelter when it's night
Where we can sleep at last, can eat, can rest.

Death is an angel whose magnetic hand
10   Drops dreams, drops sleep's seductive ecstasy;
And makes the bed of naked poverty.

Death is the poor man's purse and fatherland,
A gate that gives on fields no man has trod,
A granary that's numinous with God.

(1967)

ULICK O'CONNOR (1929–)

Ulick O'Connor lives and works in Ireland. He has published three collections of verse and had several plays presented at the Abbey Theatre.

The End of the Day   CXXIV

Beneath a thin sun
Life writhes without reason
Moves shamelessly, runs,
Till on the horizon

Comes sensuous night,
And as hunger eases
Shame takes its flight,
The poet says 'Oh Jesus

My spirits oppress me,
10   My back cries for respite,
Though dark dreams enmesh me

I will roll with delight
In the curtain of night,
Whose shades will refresh me.'

(1995)

RICHARD HOWARD

A Strange Man's Dream   CXXV
to Nadar

Have you felt – I have – a pain that you enjoyed?
Do they say about you, too: 'How strange he is!'
– I was dying, and a special agony
filled my eager soul: dread and desire,

anguish and expectation – no sense of revolt.
The closer I came to what would be the end,
the sharper was my torment and the more welcome;
my heart was wrenching free from the usual world.

I was like a child in front of a stage,
10   hating the curtain as if it were in the way . . .
Finally the cold truth was revealed:

I had simply died, and the terrible dawn
enveloped me. Could this be all there is?
The curtain was up, and I was waiting still.

(1982)

F. P. STURM

Several translators have tried their hands at 'Le Voyage', the great but long and taxing poem which Baudelaire wrote to conclude the 1861 version of *Les Fleurs du Mal*. Its combination of the colloquial and the sweeping, of lyricism, eloquence and invective, is extremely difficult to capture. In the end Sturm's version, the earliest, is also the most consistently successful.

The Voyage   CXXVI

i

The world is equal to the child's desire
Who plays with pictures by his nursery fire –
How vast the world by lamplight seems! How small
When memory's eyes look back, remembering all! –

One morning we set forth with thoughts aflame,
Or heart o'erladen with desire or shame;
And cradle, to the song of surge and breeze,
Our own infinity on the finite seas.

Some flee the memory of their childhood's home;
And others flee their fatherland; and some,
Star-gazers drowned within a woman's eyes,
Flee from the tyrant Circe's witcheries;

And, lest they still be changed to beasts, take flight
For the embrasured heavens, and space, and light,
Till one by one the stains her kisses made
In biting cold and burning sunlight fade.

But the true voyagers are they who part
From all they love because a wandering heart
Drives them to fly the Fate they cannot fly;
20   Whose call is ever 'On!' – they know not why.

Their thoughts are like the clouds that veil a star;
They dream of change as warriors dream of war;
And strange wild wishes never twice the same:
Desires no mortal man can give a name.

ii

We are like whirling tops and rolling balls –
For even when the sleepy night-time falls,
Old Curiosity still thrusts us on,
Like the cruel Angel who goads forth the sun.

The end of fate fades ever through the air,
30   And, being nowhere, may be anywhere
Where a man runs, hope waking in his breast,
For ever like a madman, seeking rest.

Our souls are wandering ships outweariëd;
And one upon the bridge asks: 'What's ahead?'
The topman's voice with an exultant sound
Cries: 'Love and Glory!' – then we run aground.

Each isle the pilot signals when 'tis late,
Is El Dorado, promised us by fate –
Imagination, spite of her belief,
40   Finds, in the light of dawn, a barren reef.

Oh the poor seeker after lands that flee!
Shall we not bind and cast into the sea
This drunken sailor whose ecstatic mood
Makes bitterer still the water's weary flood?

Such is an old tramp wandering in the mire,
Dreaming the paradise of his own desire,
Discovering cities of enchanted sleep
Where'er the light shines on a rubbish heap.

iii

Strange voyagers, what tales of noble deeds
50 Deep in your dim sea-weary eyes one reads!
Open the casket where your memories are,
And show each jewel, fashioned from a star;

For I would travel without sail or wind,
And so, to lift the sorrow from my mind,
Let your long memories of sea-days far fled
Pass o'er my spirit like a sail outspread.

What have you seen?

iv

                    'We have seen waves and stars,
And lost sea-beaches, and known many wars,
And notwithstanding war and hope and fear,
60 We were as weary there as we are here.

'The lights that on the violet sea poured down,
The suns that set behind some far-off town,
Lit in our hearts the unquiet wish to fly
Deep in the glimmering distance of the sky;

'The loveliest countries that rich cities bless,
Never contained the strange wild loveliness
By fate and chance shaped from the floating cloud –
And we were always sorrowful and proud!

'Desire from joy gains strength in weightier measure.
70   Desire, old tree who draw'st thy sap from pleasure,
Though thy bark thickens as the years pass by,
Thine arduous branches rise towards the sky;

'And wilt thou still grow taller, tree more fair
Than the tall cypress?
                    – Thus have we, with care,
'Gathered some flowers to please your eager mood,
Brothers who dream that distant things are good!

'We have seen many a jewel-glimmering throne;
And bowed to Idols when wild horns were blown
In palaces whose faery pomp and gleam
80   To your rich men would be a ruinous dream;

'And robes that were a madness to the eyes;
Women whose teeth and nails were stained with dyes;
Wise jugglers round whose neck the serpent winds –'

v

And then, and then what more?

vi

                              'O childish minds!

'Forget not that which we found everywhere,
From top to bottom of the fatal stair,
Above, beneath, around us and within,
The weary pageant of immortal sin.

'We have seen woman, stupid slave and proud,
90   Before her own frail, foolish beauty bowed;
And man, a greedy, cruel lascivious fool,
Slave of the slave, a ripple in a pool;

'The martyr's groan, the headsman's merry mood;
And banquets seasoned and perfumed with blood;
Poison, that gives the tyrant's power the slip;
And nations amorous of the brutal whip;

'Many religions not unlike our own,
All in full flight for heaven's resplendent throne;
And Sanctity, seeking delight in pain,
100   Like a sick man of his own sickness vain;

'And mad mortality, drunk with its own power,
As foolish now as in a bygone hour,
Shouting, in presence of the tortured Christ:
"I curse thee, mine own Image sacrificed."

'And silly monks in love with Lunacy,
Fleeing the troops herded by destiny,
Who seek for peace in opiate slumber furled –
Such is the pageant of the rolling world!'

vii

O bitter knowledge that the wanderers gain!
110   The world says our own age is little and vain;
For ever, yesterday, to-day, to-morrow,
'Tis horror's oasis in the sands of sorrow.

Must we depart? If you can rest, remain;
Part, if you must. Some fly, some cower in vain,
Hoping that Time, the grim and eager foe,
Will pass them by; and some run to and fro

Like the Apostles or the Wandering Jew;
Go where they will, the Slayer goes there too!
And there are some, and these are of the wise,
120 Who die as soon as birth has lit their eyes.

But when at length the Slayer treads us low,
We will have hope and cry, ' 'Tis time to go!'
As when of old we parted for Cathay
With wind-blown hair and eyes upon the bay.

We will embark upon the Shadowy Sea,
Like youthful wanderers for the first time free –
Hear you the lovely and funereal voice
That sings: *O come all ye whose wandering joys*
Are set upon the scented Lotus flower,
130 *For here we sell the fruit's miraculous boon:*
Come ye and drink the sweet and sleepy power
Of the enchanted, endless afternoon.

viii

O Death, old Captain, it is time, put forth!
We have grown weary of the gloomy north;
Though sea and sky are black as ink, lift sail!
Our hearts are full of light and will not fail.

O pour thy sleepy poison in the cup!
The fire within the heart so burns us up
That we would wander Hell and Heaven through,
140 Deep in the Unknown seeking something *new*!

(1906)

Les Epaves

From the Wreck

F. P. STURM

The original title is 'Coucher du Soleil Romantique'.

Sunset   I

    Fair is the sun when first he flames above,
       Flinging his joy down in a happy beam;
    And happy he who can salute with love
       The sunset far more glorious than a dream.

    Flower, stream, and furrow! – I have seen them all
       In the sun's eye swoon like one trembling heart –
    Though it be late let us with speed depart
       To catch at least one last ray ere it fall!

    But I pursue the fading god in vain,
10   For conquering Night makes firm her dark domain,
       Mist and gloom fall, and terrors glide between,

    And graveyard odours in the shadow swim,
    And my faint footsteps on the marsh's rim,
       Bruise the cold snail and crawling toad unseen.

(1906)

ALDOUS HUXLEY (1894–1963)

Huxley is now scarcely thought of as a poet, yet he produced five collections of verse. Three of them were published at the very outset of his literary career; but by the time the final one (*Cicadas*, 1931) appeared, his reputation as a novelist was well established. His verse shows Symbolist influences.

Lesbians III
(DELPHINE AND HIPPOLYTA)

The lamps had languisht and their light was pale;
On cushions deep Hippolyta reclined.
Those potent kisses that had torn the veil
From her young candour filled her dreaming mind.

With tempest-troubled eyes she sought the blue
Heaven of her innocence, how far away!
Like some sad traveller, who turns to view
The dim horizons passed at dawn of day.

Tears and the muffled light of weary eyes,
10   The stupor and the full voluptuous trance,
Limp arms, like weapons dropped by one who flies –
All served her fragile beauty to enhance.

Calm at her feet and joyful, Delphine lay
And gazed at her with ardent eyes and bright,
Like some strong beast that, having mauled its prey,
Draws back to mark the imprint of its bite.

Strong and yet bowed, superbly on her knees,
She snuffed her triumph, on that frailer grace
Poring voluptuously, as though to seize
20   The signs of thanks upon the other's face.

Gazing, she sought in her pale victim's eye
The speechless canticle that pleasure sings,
The infinite gratitude that, like a sigh,
Mounts slowly from the spirit's deepest springs.

'Now, now you understand (for love like ours
Is proof enough) that 'twere a sin to throw
The sacred holocaust of your first flowers
To those whose breath might parch them as they blow.

Light falls my kiss, as the ephemeral wing
30   That scarcely stirs the shining of a lake.
What ruinous pain your lover's kiss would bring!
A plough that leaves a furrow in its wake.

Over you, like a herd of ponderous kine,
Man's love will pass and his caresses fall
Like trampling hooves. Then turn your face to mine;
Turn, oh my heart, my half of me, my all!

Turn, turn, that I may see their starry lights,
Your eyes of azure; turn. For one dear glance
I will reveal love's most obscure delights,
40   And you shall drowse in pleasure's endless trance.'

'Not thankless, nor repentant in the least
Is your Hippolyta.' She raised her head.
'But one who from some grim nocturnal feast
Returns at dawn feels less disquieted.

I bear a weight of terrors, and dark hosts
Of phantoms haunt my steps and seem to lead.
I walk, compelled, behind those beckoning ghosts
Down sliding roads and under skies that bleed.

Is ours so strange an act, so full of shame?
50   Explain the terrors that disturb my bliss.
When you say, Love, I tremble at the name;
And yet my mouth is thirsty for your kiss.

Ah, look not so, dear sister, look not so!
You whom I love, even though that love should be
A snare for my undoing, even though
Loving I am lost for all eternity.'

Delphine looked up, and fate was in her eye.
From the god's tripod and beneath his spell,
Shaking her tragic locks, she made reply:
60   'Who in love's presence dares to speak of hell?

Thinker of useless thoughts, let him be cursed,
Who in his folly, venturing to vex
A question answerless and barren, first
With wrong and right involved the things of sex!

He who in mystical accord conjoins
Shadow with heat, dusk with the noon's high fire,
Shall never warm the palsy of his loins
At that red sun which mortals call desire.

Go, seek some lubber groom's deflowering lust;
70   Take him your heart and leave me here despised!
Go – and bring back, all horror and disgust,
The livid breasts man's love has stigmatized.

One may not serve two masters here below.'
But the child answered: 'I am torn apart,
I feel my inmost being rent, as though
A gulf had yawned – the gulf that is my heart.

Naught may this monster's desperate thirst assuage, –
As fire 'tis hot, as space itself profound –
Naught stay the Fury from her quenchless rage,
80   Who with her torch explores its bleeding wound.

Curtain the world away and let us try
If lassitude will bring the boon of rest.
In your deep bosom I would sink and die,
Would find the grave's fresh coolness on your breast.'

Hence, lamentable victims, get you hence!
Hells yawn beneath, your road is straight and steep.
Where all the crimes receive their recompense
Wind-whipped and seething in the lowest deep

With a huge roaring as of storms and fires,
90   Go down, mad phantoms, doomed to seek in vain
The ne'er-won goal of unassuaged desires,
And in your pleasures find eternal pain!

Sunless your caverns are; the fever damps
That filter in through every crannied vent
Break out with marsh-fire into sudden lamps
And steep your bodies with their frightful scent.

The barrenness of pleasures harsh and stale
Makes mad your thirst and parches up your skin;
And like an old flag volleying in the gale,
100   Your whole flesh shudders in the blasts of sin.

Far from your kind, outlawed and reprobate,
Go, prowl like wolves through desert worlds apart!
Disordered souls, fashion your own dark fate,
And flee the god you carry in your heart.

(1929)

PHILIP LARKIN (1922–85)

This version of the first four stanzas of 'Femmes Damnées', not published until 1978, was written in 1943 in the assumed character of 'Brunette Coleman', an imaginary poetess and novelist of the Angela Brazil school, some of whose other 'works' suggest a hearty boarding-school sapphism. These verses offer a complex blend of parody and genuine expression: for the erotically charged atmosphere of the original, Larkin has substituted a dowdy suburban setting much closer to his own later poetic territory.

Femmes Damnées   III

The fire is ash: the early morning sun
Outlines the patterns on the curtains, drawn
The night before. The milk's been on the step,
The *Guardian* in the letter-box, since dawn.

Upstairs, the beds have not been touched, and thence
Builders' estates and the main road are seen,
With labourers, petrol-pumps, a Green Line bus,
And plots of cabbages set in between.

But the living-room is ruby: there upon
10   Cushions from Harrods, strewn in tumbled heaps
Around the floor, smelling of smoke and wine,
Rosemary sits. Her hands are clasped. She weeps.

She stares about her: round the decent walls
(The ribbon lost, her pale gold hair falls down)
Sees books and photos: 'Dance'; 'The Rhythmic Life';
Miss Rachel Wilson in a cap and gown.

Stretched out before her, Rachel curls and curves,
Eyelids and lips apart, her glances filled
With satisfied ferocity; she smiles,
20   As beasts smile on the prey they have just killed.

The marble clock has stopped. The curtained sun
Burns on: the room grows hot. There, it appears,
A vase of flowers has spilt, and soaked away.
The only sound heard is the sound of tears.

(1943)

DONALD JUSTICE (1925–)

Justice studied composition with Carl Ruggles before devoting himself
to literature; he taught at a number of universities, most recently at
the University of Florida, his home state. Nineteenth-century French
poetry, in particular the works of Baudelaire and Laforgue, has been
an abiding influence on his work, both directly and mediated through
Stevens (he has been referred to as Stevens's 'supreme heir'). *A Donald
Justice Reader* (1991), a selection of poetry and short prose pieces from
throughout his career, includes previously uncollected material such as
this 1955 translation.

The Metamorphoses of a Vampire   VI

The woman, meanwhile, from her strawberry mouth –
Twisting and turning like a snake on coals,
And kneading her breasts against her corset-stays –
Let flow these words, all interfused with musk:
'My lips are moist; and I know how to make
A man forget all conscience deep in bed.
I dry all tears on my triumphant breasts
And set old men to laughing like young boys.
For those who see me naked and unveiled,
10   I take the place of sun, and moon, and stars!
I am, dear scholar, so well schooled in pleasure
That when I smother a man in my smooth arms
Or when I abandon to his teeth my bosom –
Shy and voluptuous, tender and robust –
Upon these cushions groaning with delight,
The impotent angels would damn themselves for me!'

When she had sucked the marrow from my bones,
And, languidly, I turned towards her intending
A love-kiss in return, I saw there only
20   A sort of leathery wineskin filled with pus!
I shut my eyes in a cold fright, and when
I opened them again to the good day,
Beside me lay no mannequin whose power
Seemed to have come from drinking human blood:
There trembled a confusion of old bones
Which creaked in turning like a weathervane,
Or like a signboard on an iron pole
Swung by the wind through the long winter nights.

                                                    (1955)

Galanteries, Pièces Diverses

Poetic Compliments, Various Pieces

EDNA ST VINCENT MILLAY

The Unforeseen

Harpagon, sitting up beside his father's bed,
Mused, as the breathing altered and the lips went gray,
'I've plenty of old planks, I think, out in the shed;
    I saw them there the other day.'

Célimène coos and says, 'How beautiful I am!
God, since my heart is kind, has made me fair, as well!'
Her heart! – as tough as leather, her heart! – smoked like ham;
    And turning on a spit in hell!

A sputtering gazetteer, who thinks he casts a light,
10 Says to his readers drowned in paradox and doubt,
'Where do you see him, then, this God of Truth and Right?
    This Saviour that you talk about?'

Better than these I know – although I know all three –
That foppish libertine, who yawns in easy grief
Nightly upon my shoulder, 'All right, you wait and see;
    I'm turning over a new leaf!'

The clock says, 'The condemned is ready; you may call
For him; I have advised in vain as to those flaws
Which threatened; Man is blind, deaf, fragile – like a wall
20   In which an insect lives and gnaws.'

Whereat a Presence, stranger to few, greeted by none,
Appears. 'Well met!' he mocks; 'have I not seen you pass
Before my sacred vessel, in communion
    Of joyousness, at the Black Mass?

'Each of you builds in secret a temple to my fame;
Each one of you in secret has kissed my foul behind;
Look at me; hear this laughter: *Satan* is my name, –
   Lewd, monstrous as the world! Oh, blind,

'Oh, hypocritical men! – and did you think indeed
30 To mock your master? – trick him till double wage be given?
Did it seem likely two such prizes be decreed:
   To be so rich – and enter Heaven?

'The game must pay the hunter; the hunter for his prey
Lies chilled and cramped so long behind the vain decoy;
Down through the thickness now I carry you away,
   Companions of my dreary joy;

'Down through the thickness of primeval earth and rock,
Thickness of human ashes helter-skelter blown,
Into a palace huge as I, – a single block –
40   And of no soft and crumbling stone! –

'For it is fashioned whole from Universal Sin;
And it contains my grief, my glory and my pride!'
– Meantime, from his high perch above our earthly din,
   An Angel sounds the victory wide

Of those whose heart says, 'Blessèd be this punishment,
O Lord! O Heavenly Father, be this anguish blest!
My soul in Thy kind hands at last is well content,
   A toy no more; Thou knowest best!'

So sweetly, so deliciously that music flows
50 Through the cool harvest evenings of these celestial days,
That like an ecstasy it penetrates all those
   Of whose pure lives it sings the praise.

(1936)

DICK DAVIS (1945–   )

Davis, who teaches Persian at Ohio State University, has published translations from Persian and Italian as well as several volumes of his own poetry.

The Ransom   XIX

Man must, to pay his ransom, till
Two dark, rich fields through every season;
The blade that cuts the clay is Reason
Subservient to his patient will.

To make the least rose open there
Or wheat extend its meagre ears
He irrigates with grimy tears
The stubborn fields of his despair:

The one is Art, the other Love;
10   And when the law demands he pay
The ransom due on Judgement Day
Nothing will move the Judge above

But grain heaped in His granary,
And flowers whose loveliness is such
Their mingled forms and colours touch
The angels' hearts to clemency.

(1984)

RICHARD HOWARD

To a Malabar Girl   XX

Your feet are agile as your hands; your hips
make well-endowed white women envious;
your velvet eyes are blacker than your flesh,
and for the artist pondering his theme
your body is a blessing undisguised.
Livening hot blue landscapes where you live,
you fill the water-jugs and perfume jars,
you light your master's pipe and wave away
mosquitoes from his bed – such are your tasks,
and when the plane-trees rustle in the dawn
you buy bananas ripe from the bazaar.
The day is filled with the sound of your bare feet
and snatches of incomprehensible songs;
when evening's scarlet mantle falls, you stretch
your limbs out on the matting, and you dream –
what do you dream? There must be hummingbirds
and bright hibiscus lovely as yourself . . .

Poor happy child! You want to visit France,
that crowded country where no one is well?
Make your farewells to swaying tamarinds
and trust your life to sailors and the sea?
Dressed in nothing but those muslin rags
you'd shiver out your days beneath the snow –
how you would weep for carefree nakedness,
your supple body cruelly corseted
as you hustled supper in the city's mud,

selling the fragrance of your foreign charms,
sad-eyed and yearning through our filthy fogs
for the scattered ghosts of absent coco palms!

(1982)

DONALD JUSTICE

A new title and the substitution of past for present tense effect a deliberate
distancing in this very free version of 'A une Malabaraise'. The last line
recalls the '*cocotiers absents de la superbe Afrique*' in 'Le Cygne'.

Nineteenth Century Portrait   XX

Under skies God Himself must have painted blue
    You came with your basket from the marketplace,
Bananas and a few ripe pineapples in it for the Boss.

Your skirt, all scarlet, and swinging with each step,
    Was like the bright cape matadors show the bull;
The same cloth wound about your forehead, a richly bled
    bandage.

The morning of the world sat in its palm branch,
    A just escaped parrot. Big mosquitoes hummed.
White men smoked on their verandas, each safe in his own
    small cloud.

And I imagine the straw mat you woke from;
    Your dreams, too, all hummingbirds and hibiscus;
And everything I imagine is like you, simple and fresh.

I think you must have wanted to see the States,
And even then our cities were too crowded.
Down by the docks, in winter, the cold fogs could not have
hidden

The truth from you very long. Fate was the rags
You stood shivering in, under the lampposts,
Above which must have risen, sometimes, tall ghosts of absent
palms.

(1955)

Poems added in 1868

LEWIS PIAGET SHANKS

L'Avertisseur   [v]

each man who is a man must know
that yellow serpent in his heart,
ruling as on a throne apart,
that, when he says 'I will!' cries 'No!'

plunge in the fixed and frozen lies
of Satyr-maids' or nixies' eyes,
the Fang says: 'duty, not delight!'

engender children, plant a tree,
carve Paros, chisel poetry,
10   the Fang says: 'if thou die tonight?'

whatever plan or hope we grasp,
we cannot live one moment and
avoid the warning reprimand
of that intolerable asp.

(1926)

Recueillement

This late sonnet offers a strange but intensely memorable mixture of
conventional poetic diction ('*des mortels la multitude vile*'; the mysterious
personifications) with familiar homely language. '*Sois sage*', '*tiens-toi plus
tranquille*', '*donne-moi la main*,' '*viens par ici*' are all expressions that a
mother or nurse might use in speaking to a child. Baudelaire shows his
mastery of the rhythmic patterns of the alexandrine, while at the

same time violently dislocating the conventional sonnet form with an *enjambement* across the *volta*.

Recueillement   [VI]

> *Sois sage, ô ma Douleur, et tiens-toi plus tranquille.*
> *Tu réclamais le Soir; il descend; le voici:*
> *Une atmosphère obscure enveloppe la ville,*
> *Aux uns portant la paix, aux autres le souci.*
>
> *Pendant que des mortels la multitude vile,*
> *Sous le fouet du Plaisir, ce bourreau sans merci,*
> *Va cueillir des remords dans la fête servile,*
> *Ma Douleur, donne-moi la main; viens par ici,*
>
> *Loin d'eux. Vois se pencher les défuntes Années,*
> *Sur les balcons du ciel, en robes surannées;*
> *Surgir du fond des eaux le Regret souriant;*
>
> *Le Soleil moribond s'endormir sous une arche,*
> *Et, comme un long linceul traînant à l'Orient,*
> *Entends, ma chère, entends la douce Nuit qui marche.*

10

LORD ALFRED DOUGLAS

Sois Sage O Ma Douleur   [VI]

Peace, be at peace, O thou my heaviness,
Thou calledst for the evening, lo! 'tis here,
The City wears a sombre atmosphere
That brings repose to some, to some distress.
Now while the heedless throng make haste to press

Where pleasure drives them, ruthless charioteer,
To pluck the fruits of sick remorse and fear,
Come thou with me, and leave their fretfulness.

See how they hang from heaven's high balconies,
The old lost years in faded garments dressed,
And see Regret with faintly smiling mouth;
And while the dying sun sinks in the west,
Hear how, far off, Night walks with velvet tread,
And her long robe trails all about the south.

(1909)

FRANCES CORNFORD

Meditation   [VI]

Cease, O my Sorrow, like a child be still.
You begged for evening; evening, look, is there:
The streets with an enfolding darkness fill
Which brings to this man peace, to that one, care.

Whilst Pleasure, whip in air, with brutal thong
Goads round his fair-ground, base humanity
To gather up remorse – an abject throng –
Give me your hand, my Sorrow, come with me,

Far from all this. On heaven's balcony
Lean the dead years in gowns long faded. See
Regret rise smiling from the waves released,

The Sun behind an arch sink down to die,
And like a slow shroud trailed across the East,
Listen, my love, the gentle Night moves by.

(1976)

ROBERT LOWELL

Meditation   [VI]

Calm down, my Sorrow, we must move with care.
You called for evening; it descends; it's here.
The town is coffined in its atmosphere,
bringing relief to some, to others care.

Now while the common multitude strips bare,
feels pleasure's cat o' nine tails on its back,
and fights off anguish at the great bazaar,
give me your hand, my Sorrow. Let's stand back;

back from these people! Look, the dead years dressed
10   in old clothes crowd the balconies of the sky.
Regret emerges smiling from the sea,

the sick sun slumbers underneath an arch,
and like a shroud strung out from east to west,
listen, my Dearest, hear the sweet night march!

(1961)

The Abyss   [IX]

Pascal's abyss went with him at his side,
closer than blood – alas, activity,
dreams, words, desire: all holes! On every side,
spaces, the bat-wing of insanity!
Above, below me, only depths and shoal,
the silence! And the Lord's right arm
traces his nightmare, truceless, multiform.
I cuddle the insensible blank air,
and fear to sleep as one fears a great hole.
My spirit, haunted by its vertigo,
sees the infinite at every window,
vague, horrible, and dropping God knows where . . .
Ah never to escape from numbers and form!

(1961)

LAURENCE LERNER

The Abyss   [IX]

Yes Pascal too
Whichever way he turned, saw the abyss.
Word action dream desire all come to this.
Often I've felt a chilling wind that blew
From below consciousness.

Silence below,
Silence around, above, the silent shore
The silent spaces with their fearful lure:
Hid in my dreams God shapes what all dreams show,
10   Dark symbols of desire.

I am afraid of sleep,
Afraid of it as one might be afraid
Of some enormous hole – where does it lead?
I stare through windows at infinity.
Longing for death's insensibility.
Or for a world of Form and Being, made
Not of the winds that blow from that strange deep,
Nor any part of me.

(1967)

HENRY D'AVIGDOR BLUMBERG

The Lament of an Icarus   [x]

The traffickers in shame and lust
    Still walk in pride of power and place,
But I am levelled to the dust,
    Because I dared the clouds embrace.

The stars with their flamboyant gold
    In heaven's pathway smote me blind,
So now my dim eyes but behold
    Those beacons in my heart enshrined.

In vain I hunger to aspire,
10   In vain the towering heights ascend,
Beneath some fatal orb of fire
    I feel my brittle pinions bend.

For love of beauty like a flame
    Has day by day my life consumed,
Yet none will honour with my name
    The gulf where I shall lie entombed.

(1934)

Bien loin d'ici

This curious inverted sonnet draws on memories of Baudelaire's one brief experience of life outside Europe. It has been very frequently translated.

Bien loin d'ici   [XII]

C'est ici la case sacrée
Où cette fille très parée,
Tranquille et toujours préparée,

D'une main éventant ses seins,
Et son coude dans les coussins,
Ecoute pleurer les bassins:

C'est la chambre de Dorothée.
– La brise et l'eau chantent au loin
Leur chanson de sanglots heurtée
10   *Pour bercer cette enfant gâtée.*

Du haut en bas, avec grand soin,
Sa peau délicate est frottée
D'huile odorante et de benjoin.
— Des fleurs se pâment dans un coin.

F. P. STURM

Ever So Far from Here   [XII]

Here is the chamber consecrate,
Wherein this maiden delicate,
And enigmatically sedate,

Fans herself while the moments creep,
Upon her cushions half-asleep,
And hears the fountains plash and weep:

Dorothy's chamber undefiled.
The winds and waters sing afar
Their song of sighing strange and wild
10   To lull to sleep the petted child.

From head to foot with subtle care,
Slaves have perfumed her delicate skin
With odorous oils and benzoin.
And flowers faint in a corner there.

(1906)

EDNA ST VINCENT MILLAY

Ever So Far from Here   [XII]

This is the house, the sacred box,
Where, always draped in languorous frocks,
And always at home if someone knocks,

One elbow into the pillow pressed,
She lies, and lazily fans her breast,
While fountains weep their soulfullest:

This is the chamber of Dorothy.
– Fountain and breeze for her alone
Sob in that soothing undertone.
10   Was ever so spoiled a harlot known?

With odorous oils and rosemary,
Benzoin and every unguent grown,
Her skin is rubbed most delicately.
– The flowers are faint with ecstasy.

(1936)

RICHARD HOWARD

A Long Way from Here   [XII]

This is the place – the holy hut
where, always in her Sunday best
and elbow-deep in cushions, she

waits for us – or anyone – to call,
listening to the fountains sob
and fanning her unbridled breast;

we are in Dorothea's room –
nearby, the wind and water sing
a tearful sort of cradle-song
10 to pacify this pampered child.

Dedicated downward strokes
massage her skin to burnished teak
with oil of musk and benjamin
– and all our tribute flowers swoon.

(1982)

PETITS POÈMES EN PROSE

CAROL CLARK (1940–)

Carol Clark is one of the editors of this volume.

The Stranger

1.

'Whom do you love best, puzzling man, tell us: your father, your mother, your sister or your brother?'

'I have no father, no mother, no sister and no brother.'

'Your friends?'

'Now you are using a word whose meaning to this day remains unknown to me.'

'Your country?'

'I do not know in which latitude it lies.'

'Beauty?'

'I would willingly love her, were she a goddess and immortal.'

'Gold?'

'I hate it as you hate God.'

'What do you love then, extraordinary stranger?'

'I love the clouds . . . the passing clouds . . . there . . . there . . . the wonderful clouds!'

(1997)

ALEISTER CROWLEY (1875–1947)

Crowley is today a half-legendary figure whose occult explorations and amatory predations, real and alleged, have all but erased awareness of his literary and other activities. The self-styled Great Beast, reputed Satanist, and sometime member (alongside W. B. Yeats) of the Hermetic Order of the Golden Dawn, made a prolonged study of Eastern religion and meditation, achieved a considerable reputation in fields as diverse as chess, mountaineering and big-game hunting, and produced poetry throughout his adult life. The reputation of his verse, generally privately printed in lavish editions, foundered along with his personal reputation after the Great War, much of which he had spent in America writing pro-German propaganda. His translations of the *Petits Poèmes en prose* appeared in Paris in 1928.

The Artist's *Confiteor*   3.

How penetrating are ends of autumn days! Ah, keen like pain!

For there are certain delicious feelings whose vagueness does not prevent them from being intense, and no point is sharper than that of the Infinite.

How great is the delight of drowning one's look in the vastness of sky and sea; solitude, silence, incomparable chastity of the blue; one little sail shuddering on the horizon, which by its smallness and its isolation is like a reflection of my irredeemable existence; the melodious monotony of the swell; all these things think by virtue of me, or I by virtue of them (for in the vastness of the reverie the Ego is soon lost) – they think, I say, but musically and picturesquely, without syllogisms and deductions.

At the same time thoughts, whether they arise from myself or dart forth from things external, soon become too intense. Energy in pleasure creates uneasiness and positive suffering. My nerves, too highly strung, no more give forth any but scolding and painful cries.

And now the depth of the sky affrights me; its limpidity exasperates me. The insensibility of the sea, the changelessness of the prospect, revolt me. Ah! must one eternally suffer, or fly eternally before the face of beauty? O! no, pitiless enchantress, ever victorious rival, leave me alone; cease to tempt my passion and my pride! The study of the beautiful is a duel where the artist cries with fear even before he is conquered.

(1928)

LOUISE VARÈSE (1890–1989)

Second wife of the composer Edgard Varèse, of whose early career she published an account. She was a prolific translator of French poetry and prose, tackling among others Proust, Sartre, Simenon, Michaux and Rimbaud, as well as producing a complete version of Baudelaire's prose poems (*Paris Spleen*, 1951), notable for its fidelity and vivid, straightforward tone.

The ending of this poem recalls that of 'Rêve Parisien' (CII).

The Double Room   5.

A room that is like a dream, a truly *spiritual* room, where the stagnant atmosphere is nebulously tinted pink and blue.

Here the soul takes a bath of indolence, scented with all the aromatic perfumes of desire and regret. There is about it something crepuscular, bluish shot with rose; a voluptuous dream in an eclipse.

Every piece of furniture is of an elongated form, languid and prostrate, and seems to be dreaming; endowed, one would say, with a somnambular existence like minerals and vegetables. The hangings speak a silent language like flowers, skies and setting suns.

No artistic abominations on the walls. Definite, positive art is blasphemy compared to dream and the unanalyzed impression. Here all is bathed in harmony's own adequate and delicious obscurity.

An infinitesimal scent of the most exquisite choosing, mingled with the merest breath of humidity, floats through this atmosphere where hot-house sensations cradle the drowsy spirit.

Muslin in diaphanous masses rains over the window and over the bed, spreads in snowy cataracts. And on this bed lies the Idol, the sovereign queen of my dreams. But why is she here? Who has brought her? What magic power has installed her on this throne of revery and of pleasure? No matter. She is here. I recognize her.

Yes, those are her eyes whose flame pierces the gloaming; those subtle and terrible eyes that I recognize by their dread mockery! They attract, they subjugate, they devour the imprudent gaze. Often I have studied them – black stars compelling curiosity and wonder.

To what good demon am I indebted for this encompassing atmosphere of mystery, silence, perfume and peace? O bliss! What we are wont to call life, even in its happiest moments of expansion, has nothing in common with this supreme life which I am now experiencing, and which I relish minute by minute, second by second.

No! there are no more minutes, there are no more seconds! Time has disappeared; it is Eternity that reigns, an eternity of bliss!

But a knock falls on the door, an awful, a resounding knock, and I feel, as in my dreams of hell, a pitchfork being stuck into my stomach.

Then a Spectre enters. It is a bailiff come to torture me in the name of the law; it is an infamous concubine come with her complaints to add the trivialities of her life to the sorrows of mine; it is a messenger boy from a newspaper editor clamoring for the last installment of a manuscript.

The paradisiac room and the idol, the sovereign of dreams, the *Sylphid*, as the great René used to say, the whole enchantment has vanished at the Spectre's brutal knock.

Horrors! I remember! Yes, I remember! this filthy hole, this abode of eternal boredom is truly mine. Look at the stupid, dusty, dilapidated furniture; the hearth without fire, without embers, disgusting with spittle; the sad windows where rain has traced furrows through the dust; manuscripts covered with erasures or unfinished, the calendar where a pencil has marked all the direst dates!

And that perfume out of another world which in my state of exquisite sensibility was so intoxicating? Alas, another odor has taken its place, of stale tobacco mixed with nauseating mustiness. The rancid smell of desolation.

In this narrow world, but with plenty of room for disgust, there is one object alone that delights me: the vial of opium: an old and dreadful love; and like all mistresses, alas! prolific in caresses and betrayals.

Oh! yes! Time has reappeared; Time is sovereign ruler now, and with that hideous old man the entire retinue of Memories, Regrets, Spasms, Fears, Agonies, Nightmares, Nerves, and Rages have returned.

I can assure you that the seconds are now strongly accented, and rush out of the clock crying: 'I am Life, unbearable and implacable Life!'

There is only one Second in human life whose mission it is to bring good news, *the good news* that causes every one such inexplicable terror.

Yes, Time reigns; he has resumed his brutal tyranny. And he pokes me with his double goad as if I were an ox. 'Then hoi, donkey! Sweat, slave! Man, be damned and live!'

(1951)

EDWARD KAPLAN (1942–)

Educated at Brown and Columbia Universities, Kaplan has written criticism on Michelet, Rimbaud and Baudelaire. *The Parisian Prowler*, his translation of the complete prose poems, appeared in 1989.

Une chimère, as well as the mythical monster, means a fantasy, a vain hope. Hence *'caresser une chimère'*, to cherish the dream of doing something.

To Each His Chimera   6.

Under a huge gray sky, on a huge dusty plain, without paths, without grass, without a thistle, without a nettle, I came upon several men walking along bent over.

Each of them was carrying an enormous Chimera on his back, as heavy as a sack of flour or coal, or the rig of a Roman footsoldier.

Yet the monstrous beast was not an inert weight. On the contrary, she enwrapped and subjugated the man with flexible and powerful muscles: with her two huge claws she hooked onto the breast of her mount: and her fabled head topped the man's forehead, like one of those ghastly helmets which ancient warriors hoped would increase their enemy's terror.

I questioned one of these men, and I asked him where they were going like that. He answered that he knew nothing about it, not he, nor the others; but that obviously they were going somewhere, since they were driven by an irresistible need to walk.

A curious thing to note: none of these travelers seemed bothered by the ferocious beast hanging around his neck and attached to his back. They seemed to consider it as part of themselves. All their weary and serious faces expressed no sign of despair. Under the sky's splenetic dome, their feet immersed in the dust of a terrain as ravaged as the sky, they made their way with the resigned expression of those who are condemned to hope forever.

And the procession passed by me and descended into the horizon's atmosphere, at that place where the planet's rounded surface hides from the curiosity of the human gaze.

And for a few moments I persistently tried to understand this mystery. But soon insurmountable Indifference swooped down upon me, and I was more heavily oppressed than they were themselves by their overwhelming Chimeras.

(1989)

MICHAEL HAMBURGER
(1924–)

Hamburger came with his family from Berlin to England in 1933, studied at Christ Church, Oxford, and spent the latter part of the Second World War in the Royal Army Education Corps. From 1947 he pursued an academic career in English and American universities, while establishing a reputation as an original poet and translator. His translations of Paul Celan were awarded the European Community Prize in 1990. *Charles Baudelaire: Twenty Prose Poems* (1946; revised edn 1968) is his only published collection of translations from the French.

At One O'clock in the Morning   10.

Alone, at last! Now not a sound to be heard but the rumbling of some belated and decrepit cabs. For a few hours we shall have silence, if not repose. At last the tyranny of the human face has disappeared, and I myself shall be the only cause of my sufferings.

At last, then, I am allowed to refresh myself in a bath of darkness! First of all, a double turn of the lock. It seems to me that this twist of the key will increase my solitude and fortify the barricades which at this instant separate me from the world.

Horrible life! Horrible town! Let us recapitulate the day: seen several men of letters, one of whom asked me whether one could go to Russia by a land route (no doubt he took Russia to be an island); disputed generously with the editor of a review, who, to each of my objections, replied: 'We represent the cause of decent people,' which implies that all the other newspapers are edited by scoundrels; greeted some twenty persons, with fifteen of whom I am not acquainted; distributed hand-shakes in the same proportion, and this without having taken the precaution of buying gloves; to kill time, during a shower, went to see an acrobat, who asked me to design for her the costume of a *Venustra*; paid court to the director of a theatre, who, while dismissing me, said to me: 'Perhaps you would do well to apply to Z——; he is the clumsiest, the stupidest and the most celebrated of my authors; together with him, perhaps, you would get somewhere. Go to see him, and after that we'll see'; boasted (why?) of several vile actions which I have never committed, and faint-heartedly denied some other misdeeds which I accomplished with joy, an error of bravado, an offence against human respect; refused a friend an easy service, and gave a written recommend-ation to a perfect clown; oh, isn't that enough?

Discontented with everyone and discontented with myself, I would gladly redeem myself and elate myself a little in the silence and solitude of night. Souls of those I have loved, souls of those I have sung, strengthen me, support me, rid me of lies and the corrupting vapours of the world; and you, O Lord God, grant me the grace to produce a few good verses, which shall prove to myself that I am not the lowest of men, that I am not inferior to those whom I despise.

(1946, revised 1968)

ALEISTER CROWLEY

Crowds   12.

It is not given to everybody to bathe in the man-ocean; to enjoy the crowd is an art; and he only can revel in their vitality at the expense of the human race in whom, while he lies in his cradle, a fairy has breathed the taste for travesty and for masquerade, the hatred of home and the passion for travel.

Multitude – Solitude: these terms are equivalent, and are convertible by the active and fertile poet. He who does not understand how to people his solitude is equally ignorant of the art of being alone in a crowd.

The poet enjoys this incomparable privilege, that he can be at his pleasure himself or another. Like those wandering souls that seek for an embodiment, he enters where he will into the personality of each. For him all houses are to let: and if certain places seem to be closed to him it is because in his eyes they are not worth the trouble of being visited.

The solitary and pensive stroller draws a singular intoxication from this universal communion. He who easily weds himself to the crowd becomes acquainted with feverish enjoyments, of which the egotist, closed up like a strong-box, and the idle man, shut up in his shell like a mollusc, are eternally deprived. He adopts as his own all the professions, all the joys, and all the miseries which chance brings under his notice.

What men call love is very small, very restricted, very weak compared with this ineffable orgy, this holy prostitution of the soul, which gives itself altogether, all its poetry, all its goodwill to every unexpected object, to the stranger who passes by. It is sometimes well to teach the happy of this world, were it only to humiliate for a moment their foolish pride, that there are pleasures superior to theirs, pleasures more vast and more refined. Those who found colleges, who teach peoples, missionary priests exiled to the ends of the earth, without doubt know something of these mysterious intoxications, and in the bosom of the vast family which their genius has made for themselves, they must sometimes laugh at those who compassionate them for their troubled fortune and for their life so chaste.

(1928)

NORMAN CAMERON (1905–53)

Cameron was educated at Oriel College, Oxford, where he became a lifelong friend of Robert Graves, who later edited his *Collected Poems* (1957). During the 1930s he published poems in *New Verse*, alongside Auden, MacNeice and Roy Fuller. His versions of Baudelaire's prose poems, nineteen in all, were appended to his translation of Baudelaire's *Mon Cœur mis à nu* (*My Heart Laid Bare*, 1950). Graves described him as a mixture of Presbyterian morality and Paganism: in these translations a cool precision fights it out with his intermittent affectations of diction – indeed his most striking successes are with those poems which demand a certain ironic courtliness or poeticism of tone.

A Hemisphere of Tresses   17.

Let me go on for a long, long time breathing in the fragrance of your hair; let me bathe my whole face in it, like a thirsting man in the water of a spring; let me wave it in my hand like a scented handkerchief, to fill the air with memories.

If you could but know all that I see, feel and hear in your tresses!

My soul voyages upon their perfume, as other men's souls upon music.

There is a whole dream in your hair, a dream full of sails and masts; great seas whose white crests carry me to charming climates where space is bluer and deeper, where the atmosphere is scented with fruits, leaves and human skin.

In the ocean of your hair I behold a harbour teeming with melancholy songs, lusty men of all nations, vessels of all shapes outlining their delicate and complicated structures against an immense sky on which lounges an everlasting heat.

In the caresses of your hair I recapture the languors of long hours passed on a sofa in the cabin of a handsome ship, hours lulled by the imperceptible swaying of a vessel in harbour; between pots of flowers and cool, porous water-jugs.

By the blazing hearth of your hair I breathe in the odour of tobacco mixed with opium and sugar; in the night of your hair I see the splendour of the infinite tropical azure; on the downy banks of your hair I am intoxicated by the combined odours of tar, musk and coconut oil.

Let me go on for a long time biting your heavy, dark tresses. When I gnaw at your elastic and rebellious hair, I seem to be eating my memories.

(1950)

ARTHUR SYMONS

In the Preface to his 1905 translation from the *Petits Poèmes en prose*, Symons says, 'I have tried to be absolutely faithful to the sense, the words and the rhythm of his original', and he comes quite near achieving this aim. His prose translations are far superior to his work in verse.

Petits Poèmes en prose 18 is the prose version of *Les Fleurs du Mal* LIII. Symonds has changed the tense of the first sentence: it should be 'I dream'. The 'old friend' in French has to be a female friend: '*une vieille amie*'. Later, the object which shines like a clear conscience is '*une batterie de cuisine*', a complete set not of crockery but of (probably copper) pots and pans. Otherwise the version is accurate, and mirrors the careful composition and sound-patterning of the original.

'L'Invitation au Voyage'   18.

There is a wonderful country, a country of Cockaigne, they say, which I dreamed of visiting with an old friend. It is a strange country, lost in the mists of our North, and one might call it the East of the West, the China of Europe, so freely does a warm and capricious fancy flourish there, and so patiently and persistently has that fancy illustrated it with a learned and delicate vegetation.

A real country of Cockaigne, where everything is beautiful, rich, quiet, honest; where order is the likeness and the mirror of luxury; where life is fat, and sweet to breathe; where disorder, tumult, and the unexpected are shut out; where happiness is wedded to silence; where even cooking is poetic, rich and highly flavoured at once; where all, dear love, is made in your image.

You know that feverish sickness which comes over us in our cold miseries, that nostalgia of unknown lands, that anguish of curiosity? There is a country made in your image, where all is beautiful, rich, quiet and honest; where fancy has built and decorated a western China, where life is sweet to breathe, where happiness is wedded to silence. It is there that we should live, it is there that we should die!

Yes, it is there that we should breathe, dream, and lengthen out the hours by the infinity of sensations. A musician has written an 'Invitation à la Valse': who will compose the 'Invitation au Voyage' that we can offer to the beloved, to the chosen sister?

Yes, it is in this atmosphere that it would be good to live; far off, where slower hours contain more thoughts, where clocks strike happiness with a deeper and more significant solemnity.

On shining panels, or on gilded leather of a dark richness, slumbers the discreet life of pictures, deep, calm, and devout as the souls of the painters who created it. The sunsets which colour so richly the walls of dining-room and drawing-room are sifted through beautiful hangings or through tall wrought windows leaded into many panes. The pieces of furniture are large, curious, and fantastic, armed with locks and secrets like refined souls. Mirrors, metals, hangings, goldsmith's work and pottery, play for the eyes a mute and mysterious symphony; and from all things, from every corner, from the cracks of drawers and from the folds of hangings, exhales a singular colour, a 'forget-me-not' of Sumatra, which is, as it were, the soul of the abode.

A real country of Cockaigne, I assure you, where all is beautiful, clean, and shining, like a clear conscience, like a bright array of kitchen crockery, like splendid jewellery of gold, like many coloured jewellery of silver. All the treasures of the world have found their way there, as to the house of a hard-working man who has put the whole world in his debt. Singular country, excelling others as Art excels Nature, where Nature is refashioned by dreams, where Nature is corrected, embellished, re-moulded.

Let the alchemists of horticulture seek and seek again, let them set even further and further back the limits to their happiness! Let them offer prizes of sixty and of a hundred thousand florins to whoever will solve their ambitious problems! For me, I have found my 'black tulip' and my 'blue dahlia'!

Incomparable flower, recaptured tulip, allegoric dahlia, it is there, is it not, in that beautiful country, so calm and so full of dreams, that you live and flourish? There, would you not be framed within your own analogy, and would you not see yourself again, reflected, as the mystics say, in your own 'correspondence'?

Dreams, dreams ever! and the more delicate and ambitious the soul, the further do dreams estrange it from possible things. Every man carries within himself his natural dose of opium, ceaselessly secreted and renewed, and, from birth to death, how many hours can we reckon of positive pleasure, of successful and decided action? Shall we ever live in, shall we ever pass into, that picture which my mind has painted, that picture made in your image?

These treasures, this furniture, this luxury, this order, these odours, these miraculous flowers, are you. You too are the great rivers and the quiet canals. The vast ships that drift down them, laden with riches, from whose decks comes the sound of the monotonous songs of labouring sailors, are my thoughts which slumber or rise and fall on your breast. You lead them softly towards the sea, which is the infinite, mirroring the depths of the sky in the crystal clearness of your soul; and when, weary of the surge and heavy with the spoils of the East, they return to the port of their birth, it is still my thoughts that come back enriched out of the infinite to you.

(1905)

The final passage of this poem, from 'O night!', invites comparison with XCV and CXXIV of *Les Fleurs du Mal*, and with 'Recueillement'.

Evening Twilight   22.

The day is over. A great restfulness descends into poor minds that the day's work has wearied; and thoughts take on the tender and dim colours of twilight.

Nevertheless from the mountain peak there comes to my balcony, through the transparent clouds of evening, a great clamour, made up of a crowd of discordant cries, dulled by distance into a mournful harmony, like that of the rising tide or of a storm brewing.

Who are the hapless ones to whom evening brings no calm; to whom, as to the owls, the coming of night is the signal for a witches' sabbat? The sinister ululation comes to me from the hospital on the mountain; and, in the evening, as I smoke, and look down on the quiet of the immense valley, bristling with houses, each of whose windows seem to say, 'Here is peace, here is domestic happiness!' I can, when the wind blows from the heights, lull my astonished thought with this imitation of the harmonies of hell.

Twilight excites madmen. I remember I had two friends whom twilight made quite ill. One of them lost all sense of social and friendly amenities, and flew at the first-comer like a savage. I have seen him throw at the waiter's head an excellent chicken, in which he imagined he had discovered some insulting hieroglyph. Evening, harbinger of profound delights, spoilt for him the most succulent things.

The other, a prey to disappointed ambition, turned gradually, as the daylight dwindled, sourer, more gloomy, more nettlesome. Indulgent and sociable during the day, he was pitiless in the evening; and it was not only on others, but on himself, that he vented the rage of his twilight mania.

The former died mad, unable to recognise his wife and child; the latter still keeps the restlessness of a perpetual disquietude; and, if all the honours that republics and princes can confer were heaped upon him, I believe that the twilight would still quicken in him the burning envy of imaginary distinctions. Night, which puts its own darkness into their minds, brings light to mine; and, though it is by no means rare for the same cause to bring about opposite results, I am always, as it were, perplexed and alarmed by it.

O night! O refreshing dark! for me you are the summons to an inner feast, you are the deliverer from anguish! In the solitude of the plains, in the stony labyrinths of a city, scintillation of stars, outburst of gas-lamps, you are the fireworks of the goddess Liberty!

Twilight, how gentle you are and how tender! The rosy lights that still linger on the horizon, like the last agony of day under the conquering might of its night; the flaring candle-flames that stain with dull red the last glories of the sunset; the heavy draperies that an invisible hand draws out of the depths of the East, mimic all those complex feelings that war on one another in the heart of man at the solemn moments of life.

Would you not say it was one of those strange costumes worn by dancers, in which the tempered splendours of a shining skirt show through a dark and transparent gauze, as, through the darkness of the present, pierces the delicious past? And the wavering stars of gold and silver with which it is shot, are they not those fires of fancy which take light never so well as under the deep mourning of the night?

(1905)

LOUISE VARÈSE

The exotic beauty Dorothée is also the subject of 'Bien loin d'ici', no. [xii].

The Beautiful Dorothea   25.

The sun overwhelms the city with its perpendicular and fulminating rays; the sand is blinding and the sea glitters. The stupified world weakly succumbs and takes its siesta, a siesta that is a sort of delicious death in which the sleeper, between sleeping and waking, tastes all the voluptuous delight of annihilation.

Meanwhile Dorothea, strong and proud as the sun, walks along the deserted street, the only living thing at this hour under the blue, a shining black spot in the sunlight.

She walks, swaying gently from such a slender waist set on such generous hips! Her pale pink dress of clinging silk makes a lovely contrast with the darkness of her skin, and molds accurately her long bust, the curve of her back and her pointed breasts.

A red parasol, shading her from the sun, rouges her dusky face with its blood-red glow.

The weight of the enormous pile of hair that is almost blue, pulls back her delicate head and gives her an indolently triumphant air. And the heavy ear-rings keep chattering secrets in her pretty ears.

From time to time the sea breeze lifts a corner of her flowing skirt, revealing a superb and glistening leg; and her foot, like the feet of the marble goddesses that Europe keeps carefully shut up in museums, imprints its image faithfully on the fine sand. For Dorothea is such a prodigious coquette that the pleasure of being admired prevails with her over the pride of no longer being a slave, and although freed, she still goes barefoot.

Thus she harmoniously takes her way, happy to be alive, and smiling her white smile as though she saw in the distance ahead of her a mirror reflecting her beauty and proud carriage.

At an hour when even the dogs groan with pain under the gnawing teeth of the sun, what invincible motive brings lazy Dorothea abroad, as beautiful and cool as bronze?

Why has she left her little cabin so coquettishly arranged, whose mats and flowers make such a perfect boudoir at so small a cost; where she loves to sit and comb her hair, to smoke and to be fanned by those great feather fans, or to gaze into her mirror, while the sea, pounding the shore not a hundred feet away, serves as a powerful and rhythmic accompaniment to her vague day-dreams, and exciting, aromatic odors come to her from the back of the court-yard where a ragout of saffroned rice and crabs is cooking in an iron pot?

Perhaps she has a rendezvous with some young officer who, on distant shores, has heard his comrades talking of the famous Dorothea. She would ask him, of course, to describe the Opera Ball, and also, the simple creature, if one could go to it barefoot as to Sunday dances here, when even the old Kafir women get drunk and delirious with pleasure; and if all the beautiful Paris ladies are more beautiful than she?

Dorothea is admired and pampered, and she would be perfectly happy if only she were not obliged to save up, *piastre* by *piastre*, enough to free her little sister who is all of eleven years old, and mature already, and so beautiful! She will doubtless succeed, the kindly Dorothea: but the child's master is too miserly to understand any beauty other than the beauty of his *écus*.

(1951)

ALEISTER CROWLEY

Intoxicate Yourself   33.

One must be always drunk. Everything lies in that; it is the only question worth considering. In order not to feel the horrible burden of time which breaks your shoulders and bows you down to earth, you must intoxicate yourself without truce, but with what? With wine, poetry or art? – As you will; but intoxicate yourself.

And if sometimes upon the steps of a palace, or upon the green grass of a moat, or in the sad solitude of your own room, you awake, intoxication already diminished or disappeared, ask of the wind, of the wave, of the star, of the bird, of the clock, of all that flies, of all that groans, of all that rolls, of all that sings, of all that speaks, – ask what time is it? And the wind, the wave, the star, the bird, the clock will answer you, 'It is time to intoxicate yourself.' In order to escape from the slavish martyrdom of time, intoxicate yourself, unceasingly intoxicate yourself; – with wine, or poetry, or art, which you will.

(1928)

F. W. J. HEMMINGS (1920–97)

The author of studies of Zola (1953), Stendhal (1964) and Baudelaire (*Baudelaire the Damned*, 1982), Hemmings was for many years Professor of French at the University of Leicester. In 1977 he published with a small private press a translation of eighteen of the *Petits Poèmes en prose* under the title *City Blues*. He excelled at the most 'prosaic' of the prose poems, those most clearly grounded in Parisian life and including allusions to contemporary political disputes.

This poem is perhaps the original of Oscar Wilde's famous likening of the public to Caliban seeing, or not seeing, his own face in the glass.

The Mirror   40.

A man with a hideous face entered the room and looked at himself in the glass.

'Why do you look at yourself in the mirror, since it can cause you nothing but displeasure?'

The man with the hideous face answered me: 'Sir, according to the immortal principles of 1789, all men have equal rights; therefore, I have the right to look at myself in the mirror; whether that causes me pleasure or displeasure is a matter for my own conscience.'

From the standpoint of common sense, I daresay he was right; but in law there was much to be said for his point of view.

(1977)

The French title of the next poem is 'Assommons Les Pauvres'. '*Assommer*' means to fell with blows, and '*les pauvres*' are not just 'beggars' but 'the poor'. French does not have a general imperative as English does: 'Thrash all beggars' does not make it clear who is to do the thrashing, but '*assommons*' ('let us beat up, bludgeon, finish off') suggests an invitation from poet to readers. Both title and poem are designedly shocking and the first publisher to whom it was submitted for magazine publication refused it.

Thrash All Beggars! 47·

I had shut myself up in my room for a fortnight, surrounded by the kind of books that were popular at the time (this was some sixteen or seventeen years ago): treatises on the art of making the nations healthy, wealthy and wise in ten easy lessons. I had in this manner digested — ingurgitated, I should say — all the elucubrations of these contractors for the public weal, including those whose remedy is that the poor should all accept slavery, and those who preach to them that they are monarchs unjustly deprived of their kingdom. It is scarcely to be wondered at that I was by that time in a condition bordering on vertigo or addle-headedness.

Yet I did have the impression that, locked in the depths of my brain, there lay the obscure seed of an idea that might prove superior to all the old wives' tales of which I had been perusing the catalogue from A to Z. But it was the merest ghost of an idea, something indescribably vague.

So I left my lodgings with a raging thirst, for inordinate indulgence in bad books engenders a proportionate craving for fresh air and cool drinks.

I was about to turn into a tavern when a beggar held out his hat to me, giving me one of those unforgettable looks that would topple thrones, if the spirit had power to move matter, and if a hypnotist's eye could ripen grapes.

At the same moment, I heard a voice whispering in my ear, a voice familiar to me, that of a good Angel, or a good Demon, who goes with me everywhere. (Given that Socrates had his good Demon, why should I not have the honour, like Socrates, to be certified insane by the most illustrious psychiatrists of the day?)

There does exist one difference between Socrates' familiar and mine. The former only manifested himself in order to issue warnings, interdicts and prohibitions, whereas mine deigns to advise me, makes suggestions and shows me what to do. Poor old Socrates had a purely negative demon; mine is essentially affirmative, a demon of action, a demon of battle.

Well then, this is what mine was whispering to me: 'Men are equals only if they prove it, and he alone is worthy of liberty who can conquer it.'

Without a moment's delay I leapt at my beggar. With one blow of my fist I blacked his eye, which instantly swelled to the size of a football. I split one of my fingernails to break two of his teeth. Realizing I was in no condition to knock the old man out quickly (for nature has not endowed me with great physical strength and moreover I was out of training), I gripped him with one hand by the coat-collar and with the other I seized him by the throat; holding him thus, I shook him soundly, beating his head against the wall. I should add that I had made a rapid preliminary inspection of the surroundings and had satisfied myself that in this unfrequented suburb I should be for quite a while secure from interruption by any policeman on his beat.

Having kicked him in the back with sufficient force to smash his shoulder-blades, I finally felled this weakened sexagenarian and, seizing a stout branch that was lying on the ground, I proceeded to belabour him with the steady application of a cook tenderising a steak.

All of sudden – oh wonderful! oh joy for the philosopher who finds his theory works in practice! – I saw this ancient carcass roll over and rise up with an energy I should never have suspected in so singularly shambling a frame. With a look of hatred which seemed to *augur well*, the decrepit footpad fell on me, blacked both my eyes, broke four of my teeth and, wrestling the branch from my grasp, started thrashing me to within an inch of my life. – Thanks to the strong medicine I had administered, I had restored him his pride and vitality.

Hereupon I got him to understand, using a variety of gestures, that I considered our argument to be at an end. Getting to my feet with the satisfaction that must have been felt by a sophist of the Portico, I said to him: 'Sir, *you are my equal*. Be so good as to do me the honour of sharing my purse; and remember, as you are a true philanthropist, to apply to each of your colleagues, when they ask you for alms, the same theory that I was *unhappily* constrained to put into practice on your back.' He swore to me emphatically that he had grasped my theory, and that he would follow my advice.

(1977)

MICHAEL HAMBURGER

The title of the original is in English; it is a quotation from Thomas Hood's poem about a suicide, 'The Bridge of Sighs' (1844).

Anywhere out of the World   48.

This life is a hospital where every patient is possessed with the desire to change beds; one man would like to suffer in front of the stove, and another believes that he would recover his health beside the window.

It always seems to me that I should feel well in the place where I am not, and this question of removal is one which I discuss incessantly with my soul.

'Tell me, my soul, poor chilled soul, what do you think of going to live in Lisbon? It must be warm there, and you would invigorate yourself like a lizard. This city is on the sea-shore; they say that it is built of marble and that the people there have such a hatred of vegetation that they uproot all the trees. There you have a landscape that corresponds to your taste! a landscape made of light and mineral, and liquid to reflect them!'

My soul does not reply.

'Since you are so fond of stillness, coupled with the show of movement, would you like to settle in Holland, that beatifying country? Perhaps you would find some diversion in that land whose image you have so often admired in the art galleries. What do you think of Rotterdam, you who love forests of masts, and ships moored at the foot of houses?'

My soul remains silent.

'Perhaps Batavia attracts you more? There we should find, amongst other things, the spirit of Europe married to tropical beauty.'

Not a word. Could my soul be dead?

'Is it then that you have reached such a degree of lethargy that you acquiesce in your sickness? If so, let us flee to lands that are analogues of death. I see how it is, poor soul! We shall pack our trunks for Torneo. Let us go farther still to the extreme end of the Baltic; or farther still from life, if that is possible; let us settle at the Pole. There the sun only grazes the earth obliquely, and the slow alternation of light and darkness suppresses variety and increases monotony, that half-nothingness. There we shall be able to take long baths of darkness, while for our amusement the aurora borealis shall send us its rose-coloured rays that are like the reflection of Hell's own fireworks!'

At last my soul explodes, and wisely cries out to me: 'No matter where! No matter where! As long as it's out of the world!'

(1946, revised 1968)

Epilogue

The Epilogue usually printed with the *Petits Poèmes en prose* is
in verse, and probably left unfinished by Baudelaire. There are certainly
clumsinesses of wording ('*monté sur la montagne*'; '*fleurit comme une fleur*')
that French taste of his time would have rejected. But the third and
four tercets, comparing the city to a woman and recalling the 'black'
love-poetry of 'Spleen et Idéal' (particularly no. XVIII), have un-
deniable power.

Epilogue

Le cœur content, je suis monté sur la montagne
D'où l'on peut contempler la ville en son ampleur,
Hôpital, lupanar, purgatoire, enfer, bagne,

Où toute énormité fleurit comme une fleur.
Tu sais bien, ô Satan, patron de ma détresse,
Que je n'allais pas là pour répandre un vain pleur;

Mais, comme un vieux paillard d'une vieille maîtresse,
Je voulais m'enivrer de l'énorme catin,
Dont le charme infernal me rajeunit sans cesse.

10   Que tu dormes encor dans les draps du matin,
Lourde, obscure, enrhumée, ou que tu te pavanes
Dans les voiles du soir passementés d'or fin,

Je t'aime, ô capitale infâme! Courtisanes
Et bandits, tels souvent vous offrez des plaisirs
Que ne comprennent pas les vulgaires profanes.

ARTHUR SYMONS

This version, made to accompany his 1905 selection of the prose poems, is probably Symons's best piece of verse translation.

Epilogue

With heart at rest I climbed the citadel's
Steep height, and saw the city as from a tower,
Hospital, brothel, prison, and such hells,

Where evil comes up softly like a flower.
Thou knowest, O Satan, patron of my pain,
Not for vain tears I went up at that hour;

But, like an old sad faithful lecher, fain
To drink delight of that enormous trull
Whose hellish beauty makes me young again.

Whether thou sleep, with heavy vapours full,
Sodden with day, or, new apparelled, stand
In gold-laced veils of evening beautiful,

I love thee, infamous city! Harlots and
Hunted have pleasures of their own to give,
The vulgar herd can never understand.

(1905)

ACKNOWLEDGEMENTS

Grateful thanks are due to Richard Scott Simon Ltd and Carcanet Press for permission to reprint 'Landscape', translated by John Ashbery from *A Wave*. Copyright © 1981, 1982, 1983, 1984 by John Ashbery; to Oxford University Press for 'Baudelaire in Cythera', translated by Basil Bunting from *The Complete Poems of Basil Bunting*, edited by Richard Caddel (1994); to Jane Aiken Hodge and Soho Book Company for 'A Hemisphere of Tresses', translated by Norman Cameron from *My Heart Laid Bare* (1950); to Francisco Campbell Custodio and Ad Donker Publishers for 'Voyage to Cytherea', 'The Little Old Women', 'To the Reader', 'The Irremediable', 'Correspondences', 'Elevation', 'The Thirst for the Void', 'Sympathetic Horror', 'The Possessed', 'Spleen' from *Les Fleurs du Mal*, translated by Roy Campbell (1952); to The Gallery Press for 'Correspondances', translated by Ciaran Carson from *First Language* (1993); to Hugh Cornford on behalf of the F. C. Cornford Will Trust, and Alan Anderson of the Tragara Press for 'Correspondences' and 'Meditation', translated by Frances Cornford from *Fifteen Poems from the French* (1976); to John Symonds, Literary Executor of the Estate of Aleister Crowley for 'The Artist's *Confiteor*', 'Crowds', 'Intoxicate Yourself', translated by Aleister Crowley from *Petits Poèmes en Prose* (1993); to Hippopotamus Press for 'Undulant and Opalescent the Robes', translated by Peter Dale from *Narrow Straits*; to Anvil Press Poetry for 'The Ransom', translated by Dick Davis from *The Covenant* (1984); to Nan Sherman Sussman for 'Ill-starred', 'The Giantess', 'All, All', 'The Drunkard', translated by George Dillon from *Flowers of Evil* (Harper & Bros.). Copyright © George Dillon and Edna St Vincent Millay; to Bloodaxe Books for 'Exotic Scent', translated by Alistair Elliot from *French Love Poems* (1991); to New Directions Publishing Corporation for 'Baudelaire's Music', translated by Robert Fitzgerald from *Spring Shade: Poems 1931–1970*. Copyright © 1969 by Robert Fitzgerald; to Duncan Forbes for his translation of 'Harmonie du Soir'. Copyright © Duncan Forbes, 1997; to John Fuller for 'Cats', 'Owls' (both originally published in 1954 in *Counterparts*), 'Spleen' poems (originally published in 1973 in *Tiny Tears*), translated by Roy Fuller from *New and Collected Poems* (1985). Copyright © John Fuller and the Estate of Roy Fuller; to John Goudge for his translations of 'Confession', 'The Seven Old Men' from *Selected Poems of Baudelaire*, edited by Howard Sergeant; to Random House UK Ltd for 'At One O'clock in the Morning', 'Anywhere out of the World', translated by Michael Hamburger from *Charles Baudelaire: Twenty Prose Poems* (Jonathan Cape); to Faber & Faber Ltd, and Farrar, Straus & Giroux Inc. for 'The Digging Skeleton', translated by Seamus Heaney from *North*; to Anthony Hecht for his translations of 'J'ai plus de souvenirs', 'The Swan', *Je n'ai pas oublié, voisine de la ville'*. Copyright © Anthony Hecht; to F. W. J. Hemmings for his translations of 'The Mirror', 'Thrash All Beggars' from *City Blues*; to Société Baudelaire for 'Benediction' from *The Complete Poems of Baudelaire with Selected Illustrations by Limouse*, an English Verse Translation by Dr Philip Higson and Elliot R. Ashe (Limouse Museum Publications, 1992); to David R. Godine, Publisher, Inc. for 'The Muse for Hire', 'Artist Unknown', *'Sed Non Satiata'*, 'Suppose My Name', 'Autumnal', 'A Voyage to Cytherea', 'Saint Peter's Denial', 'A Strange Man's Dream', 'To a Malabar Girl', 'The Happy Corpse', 'To a Red-haired Beggar Girl', 'I have not forgotten', translated by Richard Howard from *Les Fleurs du Mal*. Translation copyright © 1982 by Richard Howard; to Aldous Huxley Literary Estate for 'Lesbians', translated by Aldous Huxley from *Cicadas and Other Poems* (Harper & Row, 1931); to The University of Georgia Press for 'To Each His Chimera', translated by Edward K. Kaplan from *The Parisian Prowler*; to Faber & Faber Ltd and Farrar, Straus & Giroux Inc. for *'Femmes Damnées'*, translated by Philip Larkin from *Collected Poems*. Copyright © 1988, 1989 by the Estate of Philip Larkin; to Laurence Lerner for his translations of 'The Nurse', 'Morning Twilight', 'The Poor Praise Death', 'The Abyss', 'Landscape', 'Spleen' poems (Queens University Festival Publications, Belfast). Copyright © Laurence Lerner; to James Liddy for his translation of 'The Death of Lovers' from

Baudelaire's Bar Flowers (1975); to Farrar, Straus & Giroux Inc. and Faber & Faber Ltd, for 'The Servant', 'Spleen', 'Meditation', 'The Abyss', translated by Robert Lowell from *Imitations*. Copyright © 1961 by Robert Lowell. Copyright renewed © 1986, 1987, 1989 by Caroline Lowell, Harriet Lowell and Sheridan Lowell; to Oxford University Press for *'Mœsta et errabunda'*, 'The Taste for Nothingness', 'Alchemy of Suffering', translated by James McGowan from *The Flowers of Evil* (World Classics, 1993). Copyright © James McGowan, 1993; to Michael Maclagen for 'Women Accurst', translated by Sir Eric Maclagan from *The Flowers of Evil*, selected and edited by Marthiel and Jackson Mathews (Routledge & Kegan Paul, 1955); to New Directions Publishing Corporation for 'Love and the Skull', translated by Jackson Mathews from *The Flowers of Evil*. Copyright © 1965 by New Directions Publishing Corporation; to Elizabeth Barnett, literary executor, for 'Invitation to the Voyage', 'The Sphinx', 'A Memory', 'Dawn', 'The Unforeseen', 'Ever So Far from Here', 'Murdered Woman', 'The Mercenary Muse', 'Parisian Dream', translated by Edna St Vincent Millay from *Flowers of Evil* (Harper & Row). Copyright © 1936, 1963 by Edna St Vincent Millay; to Peter Riley, literary executor, and The Menard Press for 'On the Islets of Langerhans', 'After the Deluge', translated by Nicholas Moore from *Spleen* (1973). Copyright © the Estate of Nicholas Moore; to Ulick O'Connor for his translation of 'The End of the Day'; to Peter Owen Ltd, London for 'You'd Sleep with Anything', 'The Insatiable', translated by Jeremy Reed from *Black Sugar* (1992); to Anthony Ryle for his translations of 'The Sun', 'Daybreak'; to Heather Scott and Chapman Publishing for 'Gloamin', translated by Tom Scott from *The Shorter Collected Poems of Tom Scott* (1993); to Raglan Squire for 'La Chevelure', 'The Invitation to the Voyage', translated by Sir John Squire from *Poems and Baudelaire Flowers* (1909); to New Directions Publishing Corporation for 'The Spiritual Dawn', 'The Cracked Bell', 'Spleen; When the Low Heavy Sky', translated by Sir John Squire from *The Flowers of Evil*. Copyright © 1965 by New Directions Publishing Corporation; to Diana P. Read for 'Evening Twilight', 'Epilogue', *'L'Invitation au Voyage'*, 'The Two Good Sisters', 'The Beautiful Ship', *'La Beauté'*, translated by Arthur Symons (1925); to Farrar, Straus & Giroux Inc. for 'Correspondences', translated by Allen Tate from

Collected Prose 1919–1976. Copyright © 1977 by Allen Tate; to New Directions Publishing Corporation for 'The Beautiful Dorothea', 'The Double Room', translated by Louise Varèse from *Paris Spleen*. Copyright © 1947 by New Directions Publishing Corporation; to Michael Vince for his translations of 'The Enemy', 'Spleen'; to G. M. Watkins for 'I Have Not Forgotten' (from *The Listener*, 6 September 1956), 'I Offer You This Verse' (from *Selected Translations*, published by Enitharmon Press, 1977), translated by Vernon Watkins. Copyright © the Estate of Vernon Watkins; to Richard Wilbur for his translations of 'The Albatross', 'Correspondences' from *The Flowers of Evil*, selected and edited by Marthiel and Jackson Mathews (Routledge & Kegan Paul, 1955); to Harcourt Brace & Company for *'L'Invitation au Voyage'*, translated by Richard Wilbur from *Things of this World*. Copyright © 1956 and renewed 1984 by Richard Wilbur.

Every effort has been made to trace or contact all copyright holders. The publishers will be glad to make good at the earliest opportunity any omissions brought to their attention.

INDEX OF TRANSLATORS

INDEX OF TITLES

Visit Penguin on the Internet

and browse at your leisure

- ◆ preview sample extracts of our forthcoming books
- ◆ read about your favourite authors
- ◆ investigate over 10,000 titles
- ◆ enter one of our literary quizzes
- ◆ win some fantastic prizes in our competitions
- ◆ e-mail us with your comments and book reviews
- ◆ instantly order any Penguin book

and masses more!

'To be recommended without reservation ... a rich and rewarding on-line experience' – Internet Magazine

www.penguin.co.uk

READ MORE IN PENGUIN

In every corner of the world, on every subject under the sun, Penguin represents quality and variety – the very best in publishing today.

For complete information about books available from Penguin – including Puffins, Penguin Classics and Arkana – and how to order them, write to us at the appropriate address below. Please note that for copyright reasons the selection of books varies from country to country.

In the United Kingdom: Please write to *Dept. EP, Penguin Books Ltd, Bath Road, Harmondsworth, West Drayton, Middlesex UB7 0DA*

In the United States: Please write to *Consumer Sales, Penguin USA, P.O. Box 999, Dept. 17109, Bergenfield, New Jersey 07621-0120.* VISA and MasterCard holders call 1-800-253-6476 to order Penguin titles

In Canada: Please write to *Penguin Books Canada Ltd, 10 Alcorn Avenue, Suite 300, Toronto, Ontario M4V 3B2*

In Australia: Please write to *Penguin Books Australia Ltd, P.O. Box 257, Ringwood, Victoria 3134*

In New Zealand: Please write to *Penguin Books (NZ) Ltd, Private Bag 102902, North Shore Mail Centre, Auckland 10*

In India: Please write to *Penguin Books India Pvt Ltd, 706 Eros Apartments, 56 Nehru Place, New Delhi 110 019*

In the Netherlands: Please write to *Penguin Books Netherlands bv, Postbus 3507, NL-1001 AH Amsterdam*

In Germany: Please write to *Penguin Books Deutschland GmbH, Metzlerstrasse 26, 60594 Frankfurt am Main*

In Spain: Please write to *Penguin Books S. A., Bravo Murillo 19, 1° B, 28015 Madrid*

In Italy: Please write to *Penguin Italia s.r.l., Via Felice Casati 20, I–20124 Milano*

In France: Please write to *Penguin France S. A., 17 rue Lejeune, F–31000 Toulouse*

In Japan: Please write to *Penguin Books Japan, Ishikiribashi Building, 2–5–4, Suido, Bunkyo-ku, Tokyo 112*

In South Africa: Please write to *Longman Penguin Southern Africa (Pty) Ltd, Private Bag X08, Bertsham 2013*

READ MORE IN PENGUIN

A CHOICE OF CLASSICS

Armadale Wilkie Collins

Victorian critics were horrified by Lydia Gwilt, the bigamist, husband-poisoner and laudanum addict whose intrigues spur the plot of this most sensational of melodramas.

Aurora Leigh and Other Poems Elizabeth Barrett Browning

Aurora Leigh (1856), Elizabeth Barrett Browning's epic novel in blank verse, tells the story of the making of a woman poet, exploring 'the woman question', art and its relation to politics and social oppression.

Personal Narrative of a Journey to the Equinoctial Regions of the New Continent Alexander von Humboldt

Alexander von Humboldt became a wholly new kind of nineteenth-century hero – the scientist–explorer – and in *Personal Narrative* he invented a new literary genre: the travelogue.

The Pañćatantra Visnu Sarma

The Pañćatantra is one of the earliest books of fables and its influence can be seen in the *Arabian Nights*, the *Decameron*, the *Canterbury Tales* and most notably in the *Fables* of La Fontaine.

A Laodicean Thomas Hardy

The Laodicean of Hardy's title is Paula Power, a thoroughly modern young woman who, despite her wealth and independence, cannot make up her mind.

Brand Henrik Ibsen

The unsparing vision of a priest driven by faith to risk and witness the deaths of his wife and child gives *Brand* its icy ferocity. It was Ibsen's first masterpiece, a poetic drama composed in 1865 and published to tremendous critical and popular acclaim.

READ MORE IN PENGUIN

A CHOICE OF CLASSICS

Sylvia's Lovers Elizabeth Gaskell

In an atmosphere of unease the rivalries of two men, the sober tradesman Philip Hepburn, who has been devoted to his cousin Sylvia since her childhood, and the gallant, charming whaleship harpooner Charley Kinraid, are played out.

The Republic Plato

The best-known of Plato's dialogues, *The Republic* is also one of the supreme masterpieces of Western philosophy, whose influence cannot be overestimated.

Ethics Benedict de Spinoza

'Spinoza (1632–77),' wrote Bertrand Russell, 'is the noblest and most lovable of the great philosophers. Intellectually, some others have surpassed him, but ethically he is supreme.'

Virgil in English

From Chaucer to Auden, Virgil is a defining presence in English poetry. Penguin Classics' new series, Poets in Translation, offers the best translations in English, through the centuries, of the major Classical and European poets.

What is Art? Leo Tolstoy

Tolstoy wrote prolifically in a series of essays and polemics on issues of morality, social justice and religion. These culminated in *What is Art?*, published in 1898, in which he rejects the idea that art reveals and reinvents through beauty.

An Autobiography Anthony Trollope

A fascinating insight into a writer's life, in which Trollope also recorded his unhappy youth and his progress to prosperity and social recognition.

READ MORE IN PENGUIN

A CHOICE OF CLASSICS

Matthew Arnold	**Selected Prose**
Jane Austen	**Emma**
	Lady Susan/The Watsons/Sanditon
	Mansfield Park
	Northanger Abbey
	Persuasion
	Pride and Prejudice
	Sense and Sensibility
William Barnes	**Selected Poems**
Anne Brontë	**Agnes Grey**
	The Tenant of Wildfell Hall
Charlotte Brontë	**Jane Eyre**
	Shirley
	Villette
Emily Brontë	**Wuthering Heights**
Samuel Butler	**Erewhon**
	The Way of All Flesh
Lord Byron	**Selected Poems**
Thomas Carlyle	**Selected Writings**
Arthur Hugh Clough	**Selected Poems**
Wilkie Collins	**Armadale**
	The Moonstone
	No Name
	The Woman in White
Charles Darwin	**The Origin of Species**
	Voyage of the _Beagle_
Benjamin Disraeli	**Sybil**
George Eliot	**Adam Bede**
	Daniel Deronda
	Felix Holt
	Middlemarch
	The Mill on the Floss
	Romola
	Scenes of Clerical Life
	Silas Marner

READ MORE IN PENGUIN

A CHOICE OF CLASSICS

Charles Dickens	**American Notes for General Circulation**
	Barnaby Rudge
	Bleak House
	The Christmas Books (in two volumes)
	David Copperfield
	Dombey and Son
	Great Expectations
	Hard Times
	Little Dorrit
	Martin Chuzzlewit
	The Mystery of Edwin Drood
	Nicholas Nickleby
	The Old Curiosity Shop
	Oliver Twist
	Our Mutual Friend
	The Pickwick Papers
	Selected Short Fiction
	A Tale of Two Cities
Elizabeth Gaskell	**Cranford/Cousin Phillis**
	The Life of Charlotte Brontë
	Mary Barton
	North and South
	Ruth
	Sylvia's Lovers
	Wives and Daughters
Edward Gibbon	**The Decline and Fall of the Roman Empire** (in three volumes)
George Gissing	**New Grub Street**
	The Odd Women
William Godwin	**Caleb Williams**

READ MORE IN PENGUIN

A CHOICE OF CLASSICS

Thomas Hardy	**Desperate Remedies**
	The Distracted Preacher and Other Tales
	Far from the Madding Crowd
	Jude the Obscure
	The Hand of Ethelberta
	A Laodicean
	The Mayor of Casterbridge
	A Pair of Blue Eyes
	The Return of the Native
	Selected Poems
	Tess of the d'Urbervilles
	The Trumpet-Major
	Two on a Tower
	Under the Greenwood Tree
	The Well-Beloved
	The Woodlanders
Lord Macaulay	**The History of England**
Henry Mayhew	**London Labour and the London Poor**
John Stuart Mill	**The Autobiography**
	On Liberty
William Morris	**News from Nowhere** and **Other Writings**
John Henry Newman	**Apologia Pro Vita Sua**
Robert Owen	**A New View of Society and Other Writings**
Walter Pater	**Marius the Epicurean**
John Ruskin	**Unto This Last and Other Writings**
Walter Scott	**Ivanhoe**
	Heart of Mid-Lothian
	Old Mortality
	Rob Roy
	Waverley

READ MORE IN PENGUIN

A CHOICE OF CLASSICS

Robert Louis Stevenson	**Kidnapped**
	Dr Jekyll and Mr Hyde and Other Stories
	The Master of Ballantrae
	Weir of Hermiston
William Makepeace Thackeray	**The History of Henry Esmond**
	The History of Pendennis
	The Newcomes
	Vanity Fair
Anthony Trollope	**An Autobiography**
	Barchester Towers
	Can You Forgive Her?
	The Duke's Children
	The Eustace Diamonds
	Framley Parsonage
	He Knew He Was Right
	The Last Chronicle of Barset
	Phineas Finn
	The Prime Minister
	Rachel Ray
	The Small House at Allington
	The Warden
	The Way We Live Now
Oscar Wilde	**Complete Short Fiction**
	De Profundis and Other Writings
	The Picture of Dorian Gray
Mary Wollstonecraft	**A Vindication of the Rights of Woman**
	Mary and **Maria** (includes Mary Shelley's **Matilda**)
Dorothy and William Wordsworth	**Home at Grasmere**

READ MORE IN PENGUIN

A CHOICE OF CLASSICS

Honoré de Balzac	**The Black Sheep**
	César Birotteau
	The Chouans
	Cousin Bette
	Cousin Pons
	Eugénie Grandet
	A Harlot High and Low
	Lost Illusions
	A Murky Business
	Old Goriot
	Selected Short Stories
	Ursule Mirouët
	The Wild Ass's Skin
J. A. Brillat-Savarin	**The Physiology of Taste**
Charles Baudelaire	**Selected Poems**
Pierre Corneille	**The Cid/Cinna/The Theatrical Illusion**
Alphonse Daudet	**Letters from My Windmill**
Denis Diderot	**Jacques the Fatalist**
	Selected Writings on Art and Literature
Alexandre Dumas	**The Count of Monte Cristo**
Gustave Flaubert	**Bouvard and Pécuchet**
	Flaubert in Egypt
	Madame Bovary
	Salammbo
	Sentimental Education
	The Temptation of St Antony
	Three Tales
Victor Hugo	**Les Misérables**
	Notre-Dame of Paris
Laclos	**Les Liaisons Dangereuses**
La Fontaine	**Selected Fables**
Madame de Lafayette	**The Princesse de Clèves**
Lautréamont	**Maldoror and Poems**

READ MORE IN PENGUIN

A CHOICE OF CLASSICS

Molière	**The Misanthrope/The Sicilian/Tartuffe/A Doctor in Spite of Himself/The Imaginary Invalid**
	The Miser/The Would-be Gentleman/That Scoundrel Scapin/Love's the Best Doctor/Don Juan
Michel de Montaigne	**An Apology for Raymond Sebond**
	Complete Essays
Marguerite de Navarre	**The Heptameron**
Blaise Pascal	**Pensées**
	The Provincial Letters
Abbé Prevost	**Manon Lescaut**
Rabelais	**The Histories of Gargantua and Pantagruel**
Racine	**Andromache/Britannicus/Berenice**
	Iphigenia/Phaedra/Athaliah
Arthur Rimbaud	**Collected Poems**
Jean-Jacques Rousseau	**The Confessions**
	A Discourse on Inequality
	Emile
Jacques Saint-Pierre	**Paul and Virginia**
Madame de Sevigné	**Selected Letters**
Stendhal	**The Life of Henry Brulard**
	Love
	Scarlet and Black
	The Charterhouse of Parma
Voltaire	**Candide**
	Letters on England
	Philosophical Dictionary
Emile Zola	**L'Assomoir**
	La Bête humaine
	The Debacle
	The Earth
	Germinal
	Nana
	Thérèse Raquin

BY THE SAME AUTHOR

Selected Poems
Translated with an introduction by Carol Clark

This volume contains 102 poems, including ninety-one from *Les Fleurs du Mal* together with plain prose translations by Carol Clark.

'He never spoke of anything (and he spoke of the whole human soul) without showing it through a symbol, and always such a physical symbol . . . Think of his women, his springtimes with their scents, his mornings with the street-sweepers' cloud of dust . . . All the true, modern, poetic colours, remember he was the first to find them'
– Marcel Proust

'Baudelaire is indeed the greatest exemplar of modern poetry in any language' – T. S. Eliot

Selected Writings on Art and Literature
Translated with an introduction by P. E. Charvet

Les Fleurs du Mal is generally considered to be Baudelaire's major work, yet, prior to this, Baudelaire's reputation was as a critic of art, music and literature. He brought to bear the same standards on the works of others as he applied to his own: that beauty of idea and style are paramount, that art is useful if its function is the pursuit of beauty and that a quality of strangeness and originality are what make a work of art unique.

In this selection of criticism, Baudelaire's writings on the art of Delacroix, Ingres and Corot, the literature of Poe and Flaubert, and the music of Wagner, among others, illuminate not only those artists, but also the critic himself.

Intimate Journals is published in Penguin Syrens